The Tragedy of Thirteen Days in 1914. (A Review of the Diplomatic Correspondence Preceding the World War of 1914.) An Address Before the Michigan State Bar Association, June 28, 1918

THE TRAGEDY OF THIRTEEN DAYS IN 1914.

(A review of the diplomatic correspondence preceding the World War of 1914.)

An address before the Michigan State Bar Association, June 28, 1918.

BY

HORACE L. WILGUS,

Professor of Law University of Michigan

PREFATORY NOTE.

The substance of the following pages was read from notes, in an address in June to the Michigan State Bar Association The Bar Association passed a resolution providing for the printing of the same

The "notes" were not then in shape for printing, in preparing them for printing, I have quoted more fully the exact language of the documents, and in a few places made fuller statements, than were possible in the time limits of the address, otherwise the matter is the same I have made an effort to give the exact citation for every important sentence from the documents

The purpose has been to give as clear, concise, and accurate a statement,—with a maximum of the exact language used, and a minimum of comment,—of the diplomacy immediately preceding the war

At the time the address was given I had read the *Collected Documents* Beck's *Evidence in the Case*, and part of Headlam's *Twelve Days* Since then I have examined with considerable care, the most important books in the annexed bibliography I have found no sufficient reasons for changing the conclusions already formed and expressed herein I have however added a few notes based on some of these other authorities

Any one who has read Mr Beck's *Evidence in the Case*, will realize, as I do, how greatly I am indebted to him Soon after the *Collected Documents* were printed in 1915, I received a copy through the courtesy of Sir Gilbert Parker I read much of the material therein,—but was much confused by the semi-chronological arrangement by countries, which of course is the only proper official way, but it is extremely difficult to make out the connected story for all the countries, and the index alone gives but little help

Sometime later I read Mr Beck's book, and made extensive notes; I then undertook to verify them from the documents themselves, this was interesting and fascinating, but to get the full effect, I found that something like a concordance to the documents was necessary. I made one for my own use, and began the systematic study of the documents, for my own satisfaction, without thought of publication, while my conclusions are the same as Mr Beck's and Mr Archer's, they are based on my own study of the documents themselves; and it seems to me that any one with an open mind will be led irresistibly to the same conclusion by a like study

This paper cannot take the place of such a study, or of the larger works, but it is hoped that many, who have not the time to read more extensively, may find here a sufficient basis for feeling that "thrice is he armed, who has his quarrel just"

As much as possible I have used *England* for Great Britain, *Austria* for Austria-Hungary, and *Germany* for the German Empire, and also, the same instead of the name of the particular official representative of the country, when it seemed unnecessary to be more specific

In 1914, I thought it probable the outbreak of the war was due much to bungling, and Machiavellian diplomacy, by incompetent diplomats, all being much, if not equally, to blame I have been driven to the conclusion that, while that is true of the Central Powers, it is not true of the Allies, the latter, in my judgment have been represented by high-minded, able men,—Sir Edward Grey, (England), Rene Viviani, (France), and M Sazonof, (Russia), who did every thing they could honorably and honestly do to avoid war, while those of the Central Powers,—the Kaiser, Bethmann-Hollweg, Chancellor, and Von Jagow, Secretary of State, (Germany), and Berchtold, (Austria), neither high-minded, nor so able, but vicious, did everything they could dishonorably and dishonestly to pretend to avoid a war which they had deliberately planned for their own iniquitous ends,—Austria to dominate Servia and the Balkans, and Germany to dominate Europe and the world

Ann Arbor, Aug 15, 1918

SHORT BIBLIOGRAPHY

Adkins, The War, Its Origins and Warnings, London, Unwin, 1914. 227 pp

Andrassy, Count Julius, Whose Sin is the World War? New York New Era Pub House, 1915, 151 pp (Pro-Austrian)

Archer, Wm, The Thirteen Days—July 23-August 4, 1914, Oxford Clarendon Press, 1915, 244 pp (Very excellent review)

Baldwin, E F, The World War, How it looks to the Nations involved and what it means to us, New York, MacMillan, 1914, 267 pp

Beck, James M, The Double Alliance versus the Triple Entente, Oxford Pamphlets No VIII, 1914, reprinted from the New York Times, 44 pp (Best short statement)

Beck, James M, The Evidence in the Case, New York, Putnams, 1914, 200 pp (One of the very best statements, indispensable)

Chitwood, O P, The Immediate Causes of the Great War, New York, Crowell, 1917, 196 pp (An absolutely colorless account)

Collected Documents See page 15 *infra*

Dampierre, Jacques M de, German Imperialism and International Law, London, Constable, 1917, 277 pp

Davenport, B, A History of the Great War, 1914—, New York, Putnams, 1916, 545 pp

Dillon, Dr E J, A Scrap of Paper, 3d Ed, London, Hodder and Stoughton, 1914, xxvii, 220 pp

Durkheim, E and Denis, E, Who Wanted War? Paris, Librarie Armand Colin, 1915, 63 pp (Excellent short statement)

Headlam, J W, A History of Twelve Days, July 24th to August 4th, 1914, London, Unwin, 1915, 412 pp (Excellent)

Kennedy, J M, How the War Began London, Hodder and Stoughton, 1914, xxvii, 187 pp

Ludwig, Ernest, Austria-Hungary and the War, New York, Ogilvie 1915 220 pp (Pro-Austria)

Meyer, Eduard, England, Its Political Organization and Developement and the War against Germany, Boston Ritter, 1916, 328 pp (Pro-German With this should be read Britain *versus* Germany, by J M Robertson, London, Unwin, 1917—a review of Meyer's book)

Mowat, R B, Select Treaties and Documents, Oxford Pamphlets, No XVIII, Oxford Univ Press, 1914 1915, 127 pp

Price, M P, The Diplomatic History of the War, New York, Scribner, 1914, 344—102 pp (Contains many valuable documents and news paper accounts, speeches, etc. So anti-Grey as to be almost pro-German. See Archer's criticisms in Appendix to Thirteen Days.)

Rose, J. H., The Origins of the War, New York, Putnams, 1915, 201 pp.

Schmitt, B. E., England and Germany, 1740-1914, Princeton Univ. Press, 1916, 524 pp. (Excellent for many things, especially the army and navy building competition.)

Seymour, Charles, The Diplomatic Background of the War, 1870-1914, Yale Univ. Press, 1914, 331 pp.

Stowell, E. C., The Diplomacy of the War of 1914, New York, Houghton, 1915, pp. (Very careful and judicial study, with many documents, and the best chronological table of the diplomatic events.)

Willmore, J. S., The Great Crime and its Moral, London, Hodder and Stoughton, 1917, 223 pp. (Valuable.)

THE TRAGEDY OF THIRTEEN DAYS IN 1914

INTRODUCTION

The tragedy of which I shall speak this afternoon is the one that is revealed in the Diplomatic Correspondence of Europe, from July 23 to August 4, 1914, inclusive, immediately preceding and ending in the commencement of the World War The occasion of this correspondence was the murder of the heir to the Austrian throne, on June 28, 1914,—four years ago today

A very short historical review is necessary to understand the situation

Races and peoples

We speak of English, French, German, Italian, and Russian peoples, and Teutonic and Slavic races, as if they were separate and distinct races, these distinctions, however, are based more on language and nationality, than on real racial characteristics, of a hereditary nature, such as stature, shape of the head, and color of the eyes, hair, and skin Race, language, and nationality are now considered distinct things, and are rarely co-extensive, racial lines, more frequently, cut across both national and linguistic groupings Recent investigators agree that "the living people of Europe consist of layer upon layer of diverse" populations, one after another having been submerged for a time by new comers, who have in later centuries been bred out, in considerable degree, by their conquered predecessors This is so to such an extent in Europe today that "in the majority of cases, the citizen of any European nation carries within himself a mixture of every race which made its appearance in Europe," and "from the racial point of view the present war is to a certain extent a civil war"[1] Yet the history of Europe has largely been made up of the struggles between national groups—between French and German, Slav and Teuton There are today perhaps, about 94 millions of Germans in Europe, of whom 64 millions are in Germany, 12 millions in Austria, and the remainder in the immediately adjacent countries There are, too, some 140 millions of Slavs, comprising the Eastern, (Russia, Lithuania, Ruthenia), about 100 millions, the Western, (Poles, Czechs, Slovaks), about 25 millions, in a compact mass immediately adjoining the Germans on the east and north, and the Southern, (Bulgarians, Serbs, Croats, and Slovenes), about 15 millions in a compact mass south of the Danube river to the Agean sea

---

1 See Osborn H F, Men of the Old Stone Age (1915) Ripley W Z, The Races of Europe, (1899), Grant, M, The Passing of the Great Race, (1918)

Separating the east and west, from the south, Slavs, are the Hungarians, (or Magyars), about 10 millions, immediately east of whom are the Rumanians, about 12 millions,—about one-third being in Austria-Hungary[2]

Turks

In 1683, the Polish patriot king, John Sobieski, turned back the high tide of Turkish conquest almost from the very gates of Vienna It had then overflowed all the territory of central Europe from the Carpathian mountains on the north to the Agean sea on the south, and from the Black sea on the east to the Adriatic on the west

Balkans

In 1699, Hungary and Transylvania were acquired by Austria, Croatia and Slavonia about 1718, Bohemia, 1741, and Galicia by the partition of Poland, 1772-1795, and Dalmatia in 1814 Russia and Germany, or rather Prussia, had acquired large parts of Poland, at its partition, 1772-1795, and Russia acquired Bessarabia in 1812 The territory south of the Danube river and the Transylvanian Alps constitutes what is called the Balkan States They include Rumania, Bulgaria, Servia, Montenegro, Albania, Greece, and Turkey in Europe, with nearly 200,000 square miles of territory, and about 25 million people,—that is nearly the size and more than one third the population of Germany

Slavs

A very large proportion of the people in this territory are Slavs, or of Slavic descent, or of strong Slavic admixture, closely related to the Russians About 8 millions are Rumanians, 5 millions, Bulgarians, 6 millions, Serbs, 5 millions, Greeks, and a little more than one million Turks, all, however, except the Turks, have a large substratum of the Slavic blood Nearly 20 millions are Christians, more than 18 millions being members of the Eastern or Grecian church in some of its branches In addition to these Slavic peoples in the Balkan States, there are in southern Austria-Hungary, (Bosnia, Herzegovina, Croatia, and Slovania), 5 million more Slavs, (Serbs, Croats, and Slovenes), closely akin to the Serbs of Servia, while in the north of Austria-Hungary and southern and eastern Germany, there are about 21 million more Slavs, (Czechs, Poles, Ruthenians, and Slovaks) A large part of these are Catholics[3] For more than 140 years, since the treaty of 1774, Russia has claimed, and has been conceded, to be the special champion of these Christians of the Greek church, against the oppression and cruelties of the Turks[4]

Political theories

Down nearly to the nineteenth century, the political theory on the continent of Europe was that of "Government by Divine Right,"

2 See Statesman's Year Book 1915 and Encyclopedia Britannica, 11th Ed *Europe*, with maps, also map in Hayes, *Modern Europe*, Vol 2, pp 330, 427

3 See Statesman's Year Book, 1915 Encyclopedia Britannica, 11th Ed, *Europe*, and the various countries, and Hayes, C J H, *Modern Europe*, Vol. 2, pp 490-498

4 Treaty of Kuchuk Kainarji, (1774), Hayes *Modern Europe*, Vol 1, pp 386, 387, Historians History of the World Vol 21, p 419

centered in a Feudal Monarch, characterized by "absolute power," "divine authority," "hereditary right," and "private, exclusive, proprietary ownership" in the right to govern The Kaiser still holds to this doctrine[5]

Struggle for liberty

The English revolution, (1688), the American revolution, (1776), and the French revolution, (1789), were direct and successful challenges to such political doctrines Immediately following the American and French revolutions, a wave of hope of freedom ran over Europe like an electric current, this and the genius and ambition of Napoleon threatened and imperiled the absolute monarchies of all Europe In western Europe this cry for freedom demanded liberty secured by written constitutions, in the Balkan states it took, in addition, the shape of struggles to secure independence from the dominion of the Turk

Congress of Vienna

The Congress of Vienna, 1814-1815, made up of the one hundred absolute monarchs, kings, and dukes, presided over by Metternich, after the downfall of Napoleon, re-arranged the map of Europe, on the principle of the *status quo ante* and the 'balance of power' wilfully disregarding all racial and national aspirations restoring the boundaries of the reigning families using the people as pawns for dynastic aggrandizement, and providing for the suppression of liberalism It thereby blocked, but did not quench the hope of Liberty[6]

Constitutions

For the most part the struggle from 1815 to 1850, resulted in the granting of "camouflage" constitutions, by absolute monarchs, giving the shadow, but withholding the substance of Liberty, Equality, and Fraternity[7] Montenegro early obtained her independence of Turkey, and Greece likewise, in 1830, but the other Balkan states failed until 1878-1908

Bismarck

Bismarck appeared on the scene as Prime Minister of Prussia, in 1862, announcing that great questions are not decided by votes and majorities, but by "blood and iron," and in violation of the Prussian constitution and contrary to the will of the majority of the people re-organized the Prussian army[8] The next year he induced Austria

---

5 In a speech at Koenigsburg in 1910 the Kaiser said "Here my grandfather placed the crown on his head insisting that it was bestowed upon him by the grace of God alone, as the chosen instrument of heaven I consider myself such an instrument of heaven"

6 Hayes, *Modern Europe*, Vol II pp 1 118

7 For example The Prussian Constitution of January 31 1850, still in force was granted by "Frederick William (IV) by the grace of God, King of Prussia" etc In a suit in Missouri in 1876 (22 Mo 550), he says he "is the absolute monarch of the kingdom of Prussia, and as king thereof is the sole government of that country, that he is unrestrained by any constitution or law and that his will, expressed in due form, is the law of that country, and is the only legal power there known to exist as law" The Kaiser says "The supreme law is the will of the king" "That is the nature of monarchy, there is only one master and that is I"

8 Kruger, F K, *Government and Politics of the German Empire*, (1915), pp 17-18.

to aid Prussia in wresting Schleswig and Holstein from Denmark, in violation of the treaty of 1852, to which they were both parties[9] He then quarreled with Austria over the spoils, attacked her, defeated her in seven weeks, imposed $15,000,000 war indemnity on her, annexed Schleswig and Holstein, and added 30,000 square miles of territory and five million of people to Prussia He then kicked Austria out of the old German confederation, formed the North German confederation in its stead with Austria left out, drew up its constitution over night, and forced the smaller north German states into it This North German Confederation constitution is the basis of the present constitution of the German Empire[10]

In 1870, he secretly induced Russia to break her treaty of 1856 as to its Black sea clauses, in order to discredit her with the other powers[11] The same year he secretely and vigorously urged the Hohenzollern Prince Leopold, for succession to the Spanish throne, in order to stir up France, though publicly stoutly denying that the *ministry* had anything to do with it, and by modifying the Ems telegram, he deliberately brought on war with France[12] In six months France was crushed, $1,000,000,000 indemnity was imposed on her, 5,600 square miles of Alsace-Lorraine, with 1,600,000 population annexed to Prussia, and Potash mines, worth $3,000,000,000 and the greatest iron ore beds in Europe, were secured[13]

Balkan troubles

Bismarck then turned again to Austria, who had cooled off somewhat, from her treatment in the Schleswig-Holstein matter, and suggested to her that she recoup herself for her losses, by annexa-

---

9 Mowat, R B, *Introduction to Select Treaties*, Oxford Pamphlets, No XVIII, (1914-15)

10 Prussia objected to the extension of the Danish constitution to Schleswig, by the King of Denmark Bismarck, falsely representing to the Danish king that England was about to intervene in his favor, thereby induced him to remain defiant, this gave Bismarck the excuse he wanted to invade Schleswig and Holstein Many years later he said, 'From the beginning I kept annexation constantly in mind" See, Mowat, as above, Encyc Brit, 11th Ed, Schleswig-Holstein Question 2 Hayes, Modern Europe, p 186

Hanover, Hesse-Cassel Nassau, Frankfort, Hesse-Darmstadt, and Saxony made the mistake of siding with Austria in this matter, and so they were "annexed' to Prussia, or an indemnity imposed upon them See, Stevens F W, *Prussia's Territory--Where Did She Get It?* (1917), pp 1-6

11 Bismarck told the British Ambassador at Berlin, at the time that the Russian circular, denouncing these clauses, *"had taken him by surprise"* but years later confessed that he had himself initiated and instigated Russia's action—Parl Papers, 1871 Cd 245, Bismarck's Reminiscences Vol II, 115

12 See 2 Hayes, *Modern Europe*, pp 198-199 Encyc Brit, 11th Ed, *Bismarck*, Bismarck was "huffy" because King William received and talked to the French Ambassador, at Ems, concerning the candidature of the Hohenzollern Prince without referring the matter to him, and had decided to resign He had asked Roon and Moltke to dine with him, and told them his plans They were much depressed He says "During our conversation a telegram from Ems was handed to me * * * I reduced the telegram by striking out words * * * I read the concentrated edition to my guests * * * I went on 'If I communicate at once this text to the newspapers * * * it will be known in Paris before midnight, and * * * will have the effect of a red rag upon a Gallic bull' Moltke said 'If I may but live to lead our armies in such a war, then the devil may come and fetch away the old carcass'"—Bismarck's Reminiscences Vol II, pp 87-103

13 See Stevens, F W. *Prussia's Territory,—Where Did She Get It?* (1917), pp 7-9

tions in the Balkans, then struggling for independence from Turkey The time came in 1875-76, during Christian insurrection in Herzegovina and Bulgaria, repressed by such savage barbarity by the Turks as made all Europe indignant The Turks developed unexpected strength Russia came to the rescue Austria shirked After enormous expense and sacrifice Russia defeated Turkey, the preliminary peace terms were not satisfactory to Austria, who claimed that Russia's effort alone to make peace with Turkey violated the provisions of the Protocol of 1871,—entered into by all the powers, at Bismarck's suggestion, after the notice of the repudiation of the Black sea clauses of the treaty of 1856, by Russia, referred to above,—"that no Power * * * can modify treaty provisions, except with the consent of the contracting parties by mutual agreement," since Austria, Russia, Germany, France, England, and Turkey were parties to it Russia submitted and consented to the calling of the Congress of Berlin, in 1878, under the presidency of Bismarck, who, acting as an "honest broker," failed to support Russia, as she had a right to expect, because of her neutrality in the Franco-Prussian war Rumania, Servia, and Montenegro were made independent of Turkey Bulgaria was not, Montenegro was placed under the tutelage of Austria, and Bosnia and Herzegovina, while left under Turkish sovereignty, were to be "occupied and administered" by Austria Hungary In this way Russia was very largely deprived of any of the larger advantages of her great sacrifice[14] England was, perhaps, as much to blame for the final results as was Germany or Austria

The six great powers of Europe were divided into two camps the Triple Alliance between Germany, Austria-Hungary, and Italy, since 1882, and the Triple Entente, between Great Britain, France and Russia, since 1904 Their exact terms have never been fully published In 1879 Austria and Germany formed the Dual Alliance by which they mutually agreed to support one another, if either was attacked by Russia, or by some other power aided by Russia, "with the whole of the military power of their empire" In 1882, Italy became a party to it, and in 1911, claimed it was only for defensive and not aggressive, purposes[15] Sometime between 1891 and 1897 France and Russia entered into a defensive alliance, such that "the relations of Germany with Vienna were no closer than those of France with Russia" In 1899, England and Russia came to mutual agreement concerning their relations with China, and in 1907, settled all their difficulties in reference to Persia, Afghanistan, and Thibet These, however, related only to their respective spheres of influence,

14 See, Mowat, Introduction Select Treaties Oxford Pamphlets, (1914-15), Encyc Brit 11th Ed, *Europe, Berlin, Congress of*, 2 Hayes, Modern Europe, pp 498-509

15 See Mowat Select Treaties, Introduction, p lii, and pp 20, 23, also Scott Diplomatic Docs, Vol 1, pp 335, 346

and were not defensive alliances In 1904, Great Britain and France had also come to satisfactory agreements as to Egypt, Morocco, Newfoundland, and Senegambia, and thereby settling all outstanding difficulties between them These constituted "the understandings" of the Triple Entente, which was a "diplomatic group" instead of a defensive alliance, except as between France and Russia, it left Great Britain "free from engagements" For sometime, also, after 1905, French and British naval and military experts had, by authority, consulted together, but it was understood "that such consultation does not restrict the freedom of either government to decide at any future time whether or not to assist the other by armed force"[16]

Austrian coup in Balkans

In 1908 the Turkish revolution occurred Bulgaria declared her independence of Turkey Austria, backed by Germany "in shining armor," and in violation of the treaties of 1871, and 1878, to which they both were parties, annexed Bosnia and Herzegovina This greatly roused Turkey, Russia, and all the Slav states, especially Servia, which saw her hopes for access to the Adriatic sea disappear, and likewise her desire for economic independence of Austria She appealed to Russia, who protested at Vienna without avail England, also, vigorously protested at the high-handed manner of over-riding the provisions of solemn treaties Great Britain, France, and Russia asked for a conference, Germany refused to join, unless Austria consented, and she refused Germany then moblized her army against Russia, on the Polish frontier, and by a threatening autographic letter from the Kaiser, forced her to abandon her request for a conference, and assume $9,000,000 of the Turkish debt as compensation for the independence of Bulgaria Russia was so obliged to humiliate herself thus, for she had not yet recovered from the results of the Japanese war[17] Prince Bulow, then German Chancellor, says "The German sword had been thrown into the scale of the European decision, directly in support of our Austro-Hungarian ally, indirectly for the preservation of European peace, and above all for the sake of German credit, and the maintenance of our position in the world"[18]

Bitter feeling resulting

All this resulted in the creation in Russia and in the Balkan states generally, especially among the Slavic population, intensely bitter feelings, and for many years the organization of secret societies and extensive propaganda have taken place looking toward the establishment of greater Slavic states This has been particularly pronounced in Servia, struggling for a "Greater Servia," with nationalist ambitions incompatible with Austrian sovereignty over Bosnia and Her-

16 Mowat, Select Treaties, Introduction, pp lvi-lxi and pp 1-18, Collected Diplomatic Documents pp 79-82 191 Scott Diplomatic Docs, pp 623 967-969, (Eng White Paper 105 French Yellow Paper 74)
17 Mowat, *Select Treaties* pp 78-87 Chitwood O P, *The Immediate Causes of the Great War* (1917) pp 22-25
18 *Imperial Germany* pp 51-52

zegovina, and other parts of the "Dual Monarchy," inhabited by Slavic peoples. Austria-Hungary was looked upon as a second Turkey, "where the groans and tears of the Servian brother are heard, and where the gallows has its home." "The enemy is insatiable in his lusts, he holds millions of our brothers in slavery and chains. He took law and freedom from them, and subjected them all to his service. The brothers murmur and beg for still quicker help. We must not leave them to the mercy of this fearful and greedy enemy. We must hurry to their help." "We have dismembered the Turkish empire, we will dismember Austria too."[19] These were unofficial statements in newspapers and speeches, made after the declaration of 1909, whereby the Servian Government promised to renounce her attitude of protest to the annexation of Bosnia and Herzegovina, and thereafter live on good neighborly terms with Austria.[20]

MURDER OF THE ARCHDUKE

Took place in Austria

By Austrian subjects

Charged against Servia

June 28, 1914, Franz Ferdinand, Archduke, Crown Prince and heir to the Austrian throne, and his wife, were murdered at at Serajevo, the capital of Bosnia, one of the Austrian provinces annexed in 1908, about fifty miles from the Servian frontier, by two Bosniaks, both Austrian subjects, one of whom, when in Servia, had been considered dangerous, and Servia had tried to expel him, but was prevented by Austria claiming he was harmless.[21] The Austrian papers immediately charged that the murder was due to a Servian conspiracy.[22] The Servian Royal family and the Government immediately sent messages of condolence, and canceled festivities to take place in Belgrade on that day.[23] Two days later the Servian minister at Vienna, informed Austria that the Servian government was "prepared to submit to trial any persons implicated in the plot, in the event of its being proved that there are any in Servia."[24] The Austrian papers, controlled by the Government, constantly charged that the Servian people rejoiced over the murder, especially at Belgrade, Nish, and Uskub, as an act of revenge for the annexation, and as a step looking to the detachment of territory from Austria.[25] Servian officials how-

19. These are sample quotations. The first and last are from Servian Newspapers, of 1912-13, the middle one is from a speech of the President, (a major in the Servian army), of the "Sokol Society" in January 1914. Collected Diplomatic Docs., pp. 474, 475, 481, Austrian Red Book, Appendix 1, 3.

20. Collected Diplomatic Docs., p. 3, Brit. Dip. Cor., No. 4.

21. Col. Dip. Docs., pp. 27, 373, Brit. Dip. Cor., No. 27, Serv. Blue Book, No. 8.

22. Col. Dip. Docs., pp. 372, 374, 376, 378, 384, Serv. Blue Book, Nos. 8, 12, 16, 17, 30.

23. Col. Dip. Docs., p. 384, Serv. Blue Book, No. 30. Austria claims festivities were not stopped for more than 5 hours. ARB 448.

24. CDD p. 371, SBB, No. 5. (Hereafter CDD—Col. Dip. Docs., and SBB—Serv. Blue Book.

25. CDD pp. 448, 449, 450, Austrian Red Book, (ARB), Nos. 1, 3, 5, 6.

ever, claimed that "the Serajevo outrage has been most severely condemned in all circles of society, inasmuch as all, official as well as unofficial, immediately recognized that this outrage would be most prejudical not only to our good neighborly relations to Austria-Hungary, but also to our co-nationalists in that country," and that "it was of the greatest interest to Servia to prevent the perpetration of this outrage Unfortunately this did not lie within Servia's power, as both assassins are Austrian subjects."[26]

INVESTIGATION BY AUSTRIA

Results not published

A secret ministerial investigation was made by the Austrian District court, in the prison at Serajevo, this lasted for nearly a month, Servia was not notified and was not asked to participate.[27] Almost nothing was said officially during this time, the results of the findings were not published There was little popular clamor at the time, although the Austrian papers persistently charged the Servian government with complicity, at least by sufferance, in the murder, the German and English newspapers repeated these statements from the Austrian papers, to all these the Servian papers made bitter denials and counter-charges.[28]

KNOWLEDGE OF DIPLOMATS

Germany alone knew

Aside from German officials, none of the European diplomats had any direct or definite knowledge of the results of the findings at the investigation, or the probable acts or claims of Austria She studiously withheld these from the representatives of all the powers, in-

26 CDD p 372, SBB No 8

NOTE.—*The murder of the Archduke* The Archduke was a man of strong and independent will, greatly loved by the army, but almost hated by the Bosnians His political views did not accord with those of the Austrian and German Emperors, whose policy was to dominate and repress the political aspirations of the Slav population of the Austrian Empire The Archduke's hope was to appease these people, and erect them into a Slavic state, reaching to the Black Sea, making the dual monarchy a triple monarchy each state having an independent status of its own but bound to the Monarchy through the Emperor in all affairs and interests it had in common with the others. This would have blocked the Servian hopes of a Greater Servia, and also the Kaiser's "Mittel-Europa" plans The Kaiser and the Archduke were not friends, in fact detested one another, their last interview a few days before the murder, was most stormy The Archduke strongly objected to the programme of greatly increased military preparations, urged by the Kaiser and the Hungarians, to be used for subjecting the Servians by force The Kaiser immediately telegraphed Budapest of the Archduke's refusal to approve That there was a plot to murder the Archduke, at his proposed visit to Sarajevo, was known at Vienna, Budapest, and Belgrade Servia warned Austria of this, yet the Archduke was not informed, nor was any effort made to dissuade him from making the visit, nor were any effective steps taken to protect him—Davenport History of the Great War, (1916) pp 82 87

27 CDD pp 371 377, 381, 385 SBB Nos 5 16 23, 30 British and German Ideals, reprinted from Round Table 1914 1915 p 107

28 CDD pp 370, 371 372 373 374, 376 378, 379 380 382, 383, 384, FYB No 14, SBB, Nos 1, 2 3 4 7, 8, 9 11, 12, 15 16, 19, 20, 21, 22, 24, 27, 29, 30

cluding her ally, Italy,—except Germany [29] It was generally assumed that if the investigation showed Servian complicity, demands of some sort would be made on the Servian government, by Austria, but it was semi-officially stated that her claims would be moderate, and would "contain nothing with which a self respecting State need hesitate to comply" [30]

THE GREATER TRAGEDY

The murder of the Archduke and his wife was a tragedy, but in itself was not different from such as have occurred before Its awful significance is in furnishing the occasion and pretext of that infinitely greater tragedy, that for the past four years has drenched the world in blood

It is my purpose to examine the responsibility for this calamity,—mainly from the records of the Diplomatic Correspondence immediately preceding the commencement of the war At the end, I will refer briefly to some matters that are not in the official records, but are fully established otherwise

THE RECORDS

Full records except between Austria and Germany

These include the various official publications of the respective governments, of parts or all of the diplomatic correspondence, contained in the popularly called colored books or papers The British Blue Books, (BBB) (1) and (2), 342 pages, and 371 documents, the French Yellow Book, (FYB), 237 pages, 185 documents, Russian Orange Books, (ROB), (1) and (2), 107 pages, 177 documents, Belgian Grey Books, (BGB), (1) and (2), 182 pages, 198 documents, Serbian Blue Book, (SBB), 50 pages, 53 documents, Italian Green Book, (IGB), 120 pages, 73 documents, German White Book, (GWB), 90 pages, 43 documents, and Austrian Red Books, (ARB), (1) and (2), 344 pages, and 274 documents With two exceptions, these documents give in detail what passed between the Capitals of Europe during these days The two exceptions are the communications made by Austria to Germany, Vienna to Berlin, and the reverse The documents show that much communication took place between these capitals, but almost nothing of it is published in either the German White Book, or the Austrian Red Books The terms of these communications have been withheld, and are conspicuous by their absence [31]

29 CDD pp 30, 114, 158, 165, 176, 396, Brit Blue Book (BBB), Nos. 38, 161 French Yellow Book (FYB), Nos 26 27 35, 50, SBB No 52

30 CDD pp 115, 152, 395, 396, BBB No 161, FYB No 20, SBB No 52

31 There are three principal collections of these documents Collected Diplomatic Documents (CDD), London, 1915, p 561 This does not include BBB (2), BGB (2), ROB (2), nor ARB (2) BBB (2) contains correspond-

DELIVERY OF THE ULTIMATUM

Reply demanded in 48 hours

At 6 p m, Thursday, July 23, 1914, the Austrian Minister at Belgrade, handed a Note[32] to the Acting Prime Minister of Servia, to be answered within 48 hours, that is, by 6 p m, Saturday, and added that "he and his staff would leave Belgrade unless a favorable answer were forthcoming within the stipulated time"[33] The Servian

Diplomats on vacations

Ministers were absent from Belgrade at the time, the President of France and the President of the Council and Prime Minister for Foreign Affairs, were known to be at sea on their way home from St Petersburg which they had left the same night, the German Emperor was in Scandinavia, and the Prussian Ambassador at Vienna had left a few days before, on the assurance of Austria "that the demands on Servia would be thoroughly acceptable" The Italian Minister for Foreign Affairs was also away from Rome[34] The Austrian Minister for Foreign Affairs left Vienna on July 25, (the day Servia's reply was due) to go to Ischl, six hours away

CHARGES IN THE ULTIMATUM

Subversive movement against Servia alleged

This ultimatum alleged the existence in Servia of a "subversive movement," born under "the eye of the Servian government," with

---

31 . . . ence between England and Turkey BGB (2) between England and Belgium, ROB (2), between Russia and Turkey ARB (2) between Austria and Turkey Scott J B, Diplomatic Documents (SDD) Parts 1 and 2, 1916 The Times (London) Documentary History of the War Vols 1 and 2 Diplomatic (TDD), 1917 These documents are in the main arranged chronologically by countries, and are given a number by which they are cited These numbers do not exactly correspond in a few cases in the different collections The CDD were the first to be published are official and are the basis of all the others, they were published as British White Papers (BPW) Miscellaneous The BBB (1) Miscl Nos 6 8 10 Sept 1914 FYB Miscl No 15, Dec, 1914 BGB (1), ROB (1) ARB (1) SBB,—all Miscl Oct 1914 These and GWB (1) were gathered together and published as CDD in one volume in 1915 The GWB (1) was laid before the Imperial Diet August 3 1914 and published very soon thereafter by the Imperial Foreign Office, with the 'only authorized translation" into English by Liebheit and Thiesen," Berlin, the second GWB was published by authority early in 1915 with an authorized translation into English, all of GWB (1) is reprinted but the new authorized translation differs somewhat from the only authorized" one first published BBB is often cited as BWP (British White Paper), or BDC (British Diplomatic Correspondence), or EWB, or EWP that is English White Paper or Book or just E The others are also cited quite often as 'Papers" as FYP or BGP etc The TDD cites them B—BBB, G—BGB, O—ROB R—ARB S—SBB, W—GWB Y—FYB The TDD seem to have much the best index and cross-references Both SDD, and TDD have very helpful tables of contents of the separate books," giving number, date, parties and contents of each document, chronologically and page where found

32 On July 23 the Austrian Ambassador at London told Earl Grey that the Note (which he would deliver the next day) would be something in the nature of a time limit, which was in effect akin to an ultimatum" The next day Austria insisted that it was a 'demarche with a time limit" It was treated by all as an *"ultimatum"* CDD, pp 2 14, 16, 17, 18, 20, 21, 177 159 424

33 CDD, p 388, 2 SDD, 1469, SBB No 33

34 CDD, p 388, 2 SDD, p 1469, SBB No 33 CDD p 266, 2 SDD, p 1331 ROB No 1 CDD, pp 15, 154 161 165 169 171 176, 2 SDD pp 880, 1 SDD pp 568, 582, 592 594 595, 604 BBB No 6, FYB, Nos 22, 29, 41 44 45, 50, 51

35 CDD, p 23, 2 SDD, 893, BBB, No 20

the object of detaching territory from Austria, that Servia had done nothing to repress it had permitted criminal machinations of various societies, tolerated and glorified their perpetrators in the public press, and allowed officials to participate therein, contrary to her promise of 1909

DEMANDS OF THE ULTIMATUM

Austria demanded that Servia publish in her Official Gazette on Sunday, July 26, 1914, and as an order of the day to the Servian army, and in the Army Bulletin, a declaration, prepared by Austria substantially as follows — *Humiliating demands*

That Servia condemns all such propaganda, regrets that Servian officers have participated therein, and *binds* herself to—

1 Suppress every publication inciting hatred of Austria,

2 Dissolve all secret societies engaging in, and confiscate their means of, such propaganda,

3 Eliminate all such from public instruction,

4 Remove all officers guilty whose names Austria reserves the right to communicate to Servia,

5 "Accept the collaboration in Servia of representatives of the Austro-Hungarian Government for the suppression of the subversive movement directed against the territorial integrity of the Monarchy", (in GWB, this reads "Consent that in Servia officials of the Imperial and Royal Government co operate in the suppression of a movement directed against the territorial integrity of the monarchy"), *Interfere with Servian sovereignty*

6 "Take judicial proceedings against accessories to the plot of the 28th June who are on Servian territory, the delegates of the Austro Hungarian Government will take part in the investigation relating thereto", (in GWB this reads "Commence a judicial investigation against the participants of the conspiracy of June 28th, who are on Servian territory Officials delegated by the Imperial and Royal Government, will participate in the examinations"),

7 Arrest Major Tankosic, and Milan Ciganowic, officials, alleged to be implicated in the crime,

8 Prevent the smuggling of arms and explosives across the Austro-Servian frontier,

9 Dismiss guilty army and civil officials,

36 CDD pp 3, 415, 2 SDD 866 781, BBB No 4, ARB No 7, FYB, No 24 ROB No 2 SBB, No 31 GWB *Original Telegrams*, etc

37 CDD pp 38, 414-416, 2 SDD, 781, 2 SDD, 866 BBB, No 4, GWB, *Telegrams*

10 Explain alleged interviews by Servian officials, hostile to Austria

11 Notify Austria without delay of the execution of the foregoing,

12 Reply at the latest by 6 o clock on Saturday evening, the 25th July

MEMORANDUM ANNEXED

There was a memorandum annexed to this ultimatum stating that the Austrian investigation at Serajevo showed [38]

Murder planned in Belgrade

> That the murder was planned in Belgrade by Princip, Gabrinowic, Ciganowic, and Grabez, with the aid of Tankosic, that the six bombs and four pistols used, were obtained by Tankosic and Ciganowic, at the arsenal at Belgrade, that Ciganowic gave instruction in their use in a forest near there to Princip, Gabrinowic, and Grabez, that Ciganowic originated a secret system of transportation, by which, with the help of a Servian frontier captain and a custom officer, an entry into Bosnia was effected

No part of the evidence was then submitted or tendered to Serbia The ultimatum is supposed to have been prepared under the general direction of Count Tisza, President of the Ministry of Hungary, by Count Forgach, former Austrian Minister to Servia, then Under Secretary of State for Foreign Affairs, he had been in 1908-9 notoriously connected with the forged papers, on which charges of Servian conspiracies had been based in the Agram and Friedjung trials in 1909-10 [39]

SURPRISE AT THE CHARACTER OF THE ULTIMATUM

Ultimatum assumed guilt of Servia

Demand would require change in laws

The substance if not the complete text of the note, treated as an ultimatum, was immediately published in the European newspapers, before official copies were received by the Great Powers, other than Germany [40] It will be noted that it assumed guilty knowledge, active participation, and criminal complicity in the propaganda and crime charged, by the Servian Officials, and demanded immediate investigation and suppression, removal of officials named by Austria, and supervision and participation by Austrian officials in such investigation and suppression, in a way inconsistent with the laws and

38 CDD pp 12-13 416-417 2 SDD 784 877 BBB No 4

39 British and German Ideals (The Round Table Sept., 1914 March, 1915) p 107, The Britannica Year Book, 1913 p 961 CDD 396, 2 SDD, 1482 SBB No 52 FYB No 30

40 CDD 155 158 150 161 268 396 456 1 SDD 569, 579 582 2 SDD, 1338 1482 FYB, Nos 23 27, 29 29, 30 ROB, No 7, ARB, No 11 SBB, No 52

sovereignty of Servia."[41] Sir Edward Grey said he "had never before seen one state address to another independent state a document of so formidable a character."[42] Russian and French officials agreed that it was quite impossible for any independent state, however small to accept[43] and Servia "would no longer be master in her own house if she did."[44] The German Secretary of State admitted she "could not swallow certain of the demands,"[45] and all the representatives of the Great Powers at Vienna, except the German, were surprised and dumbfounded at its contents.[46]

GERMANY'S CLAIM

Diplomatic correspondence among the other powers immediately began,—before Servia replied. And inasmuch as Germany made the first move, it is proper to state Germany's claims first, and then examine them in the light of the actual records. Germany has from the first claimed, and yet claims:

1. The war is a defensive one on her part. In a speech from the balcony of the Royal Palace in Berlin, July 31, 1914, the Kaiser said: Defensive war

> "Envious nations on all sides are forcing us to a justifiable defense. They are forcing the sword into my hands."[47]

And in his speech, at the opening of the Reichstag, August 4, 1914, he said:

> "In a war that has been forced upon us, with a clear conscience, and a clean hand we take up the sword."[48]

2. Russia was responsible. The sub-title of the German White Book is: "How Russia and her ruler betrayed Germany's confidence and thereby made the European war." Russia responsible

3. She, Germany, did not know, and had nothing to do with, the contents of Austria's ultimatum to Servia. Germany not accessory

GERMANY'S KNOWLEDGE

Throughout the negotiations German officials constantly told the Russian, English, and French officials that "They had not known beforehand," were "entirely ignorant" of, and "exercised no influence on" the contents of the ultimatum, and there was "no concert," or Germany claimed no knowledge

41. CDD 13, 157, 268, 275, 478; 1 SDD 578; 2 SDD 879, 1337, 1350; BBB, No 5; FYB No 26; ROB No 6, 25; ARB, No 11; CDD, 39; 2 SDD, 917; BBB, No 44.
42. CDD 13, 165; 1 SDD 586; 2 SDD 879; BBB No 5; FYB No 34.
43. CDD, 164, 281; 1 SDD 586; 2 SDD 1358; FYB, No 33; ROB No 11.
44. CDD, 458; 1 SDD 24; ARB No 11.
45. CDD, 23; 2 SDD 891; BBB No 18.
46. CDD 158, 174, 396; 1 SDD, 579, 602; 2 SDD 1482; FYB Nos 158, 174; SBB No 52.
47. Gauss *German Emperor as shown in his Public Acts*, (October 1915), p 323.
48. *Ib.*, p 324.

"definite understanding" between Germany and Austria as to it."[49] This was false, and after the war was begun the Foreign office admitted that Austria asked Germany for her opinion, and she answered "We were able to agree with" Austria's estimate of the situation, and assure her "that any action considered necessary," by her "would meet with our approval," and we gave her "a completely free hand in her action against Servia." "We were perfectly aware that a possible warlike attitude" of Austria "against Servia might bring Russia in," and "involve us in war, in accordance with our duties as allies."[50] The time and extent of Germany's knowledge of the ultimatum, and the part she had in it will be discussed later on.

Yet gave Austria free hand

NEGOTIATIONS

Thursday, July 23, 1914

Germany forbids intervention

As indicated above, *Germany* made the first move. This was in the evening of the day the ultimatum was sent by Austria to Servia, July 23, and itself indicated Germany had prior knowledge of its contents. It was a communication sent by Germany to England, France, and Russia, and stated that "*the action as well as the demands*" of Austria, are "absolutely justifiable." "It is to be feared that the Servian Government will decline to meet these demands." There would then be nothing left to Austria "but to press their demands," "and, if need be, enforce the same by appeal to military measures, in regard to which the choice of means must be left with Austria." "We earnestly desire the localization of the conflict because any intervention of another Power, owing to the various treaty-alliances, would entail inconceivable consequences."[51] In other words, Austria must have a free hand to crush Servia, and any intervention by any other power meant European war.

Friday, July 24, 1914

Ultimatum meant war

The ultimatum reached England, France, Belgium, and Russia, about 10 o'clock,—one third of the time limit already having passed.[52]

---

49 CDD pp 14, 23 25 149 161 166, 169, 181, 196, 272 273, 2 SDD, 880 896, 1 SDD, 562 563 582 588 592, 609, 640, 2 SDD, 1316, 1347; BBB, Nos 6 18 25 FYB, Nos 15 17, 30 36, 41, 57 78, ROB 18, 19, 20

50 CDD 406, 2 SDD, 771 GWB Statement of Foreign Office, Aug 3, 1914

51 CDD, pp 16, 179 267 424, 1 SDD 579, 2 SDD, 798 883, 1335; BBB, No 9 FYB No 28 ROB No 3 GWB Ex 1 On July 21, the German Secretary of State insisted that the question at issue was one for settlement between Servia and Austria alone, and that there should be no interference from outside in the discussions between these two countries" BBB No 2 The German Secretary of State told French Ambassador at Berlin "the note was forcible and he approved it" "the question was a domestic one for Austria and he hopes it will be localized."

52 CDD pp 2 13 155 267, 300, 2 SDD, 864 879 1 SDD, 576, 2 SDD 1335, 1 SDD, 300, BBB, Nos 3 5, FYB, No 25, BGB, No 1, ROB, No 3

The English, French, Russian and German officials all considered that it "meant war", indeed that it was so "drawn as to make war inevitable", that Austria was determined to "inflict humiliation on Servia," and would "accept no intervention until the blow had been delivered and received full in the face by Servia."[53]

Russia objects

Servia immediately appealed to Russia.[54] Russia immediately declared she "could not remain indifferent," and "could not allow Austria to crush Servia," and the question was not "merely between Servia and Austria, but a European" one.[55]

Russia urged France and England to stand with her. France agreed to support her in negotiations and as an ally "if necessity arose", England refused to make such an agreement.[56]

Austria claims conquest of Servia not contemplated.

Austria explained to Russia that she desired Servia "publicly to disavow the tendencies directed against" Austria, "suppress them by administrative measures" and "make it possible to satisfy herself "that these were honestly carried out" that she "did not aim at any increase of territory," "entertained no thought of conquest," "would not claim Servian territory" and did not "intend to * * change the balance of powers in Balkans."[57] At the same time she also explained "in strict confidence" to England, that if a satisfactory reply was not received within the time limit, she would break off diplomatic relations with Servia, begin military preparations and was "absolutely resolved to carry through" her "just demands."[58]

But determined to use force if necessary

Extension of time for reply requested

Russia and England immediately made separate and joint requests, directly and indirectly through Germany, to Austria, for an extension of time for the Servian reply, to enable the powers to study the demands of Austria, advise Servia, and "smooth away the difficulties that have arisen."[59]

Request "passed on" by Germany

Germany answered that she "passed on" this request to Austria, but that the Foreign Minister was not at home, that it was probably "too late" to get "the time limit extended", that Austria "wished to give the Servians a lesson and meant to take military action," and that Servia "could not swallow certain of the demands."[60] There is no record or indication that Germany made or joined in any request

---

53 CDD, pp 38, 23, 37, 171; 2 SDD, 891, 912, 913; 1 SDD, 595; BBB Nos 18, 40, 41; FYB No 45.
54 CDD, pp 267, 389; 2 SDD, 1337, 1470; ROB No 6; SBB, No 37.
55 CDD, pp 22, 163, 269, 389, 407, 427, 439; 2 SDD, 890; 1 SDD, 584; 2 SDD, 1339, 1470; 2 SDD, 774, 802, 26; BBB No 17; FYB No 31; ROB No 10; SBB No 36; GWB Tel etc, Ex 4; ARB, No 15.
56 CDD, p 14; 2 SDD, 880; BBB No 6.
57 CDD, pp 460, 426, 15; 1 SDD, 28; 2 SDD, 801, 882; ARB, No 18; GWB, Ex 3; BBP No 7.
58 CDD, p 460; 1 SDD, 27; ARB No 17.
59 CDD, pp 18, 19, 126, 167, 171, 499; 2 SDD, 885, 887, 897; 1 SDD, 590, 595, 75; BBB Nos 11, 13, 26; FYB Nos 38, 45; ARB Nos 20, 21.
60 CDD, pp 22, 170; 2 SDD, 891; 1 SDD, 595; BBB, No 18; FYB, No 43.

to Austria to extend the time Austria, the next day, denied the request for any extension of time[61]

Saturday, July 25, 1914

Servia urged to be conciliatory

England France and *Russia* all urged Servia to give as conciliatory answer as possible[62]

Russia offers to stand aside

Russia suggested to Servia that she appeal to the powers to help her, and if she did so, "Russia would be quite ready to stand aside and leave the question in the hands of England, France, Germany and Italy"[63]

Powers request frontiers be not crossed

England proposed the "four powers,—England, France, Germany and Italy,—join in asking the Austrian and Russian governments not to cross the Servian frontier, and give time for the four powers acting at Vienna and St Petersburgh to try to arrange matters,"[64] but "unless Germany would propose and participate in such action at Vienna" it would be futile[65] "No intervention would be tolerated by either Russia or Austria unless it was clearly impartial, and included the allies or friends of both The co-operation of Germany would, therefore, be essential"[66]

Germany refuses to join

Germany refused "the matter was a domestic one for Austria", "all these *demarches* were too late", Germany "supports the claims" of Austria against Servia "as justified," and "could only be guided by her duties as an ally" of Austria, "this question must be localized by virtue of all the powers refraining from intervention", but said "we are prepared in the event of an Austro-Russia controversy, quite apart from our known duties as allies, to intercede between Russia and Austria jointly with the other powers"[67] It is difficult to understand what this last suggestion means, since she was being asked to intercede because the acts and demands of Austria, had from the first created a controversy with Russia

Austria and Germany understood war probable

July 23, the *Austrian* ambassador at London had told Sir Edward Grey, "that all would depend on Russia", and on July 25 the Austrian Minister of Foreign Affairs told his ambassador at St Petersburg "We were, of course aware, when we decided to take serious measures against Servia, of the possibility that the Servian dispute might develop into a collision with Russia" and assumed that he had already "established a close understanding with" the German ambassador at St Petersburg, "who will certainly have been enjoined by

61 CDD pp 499 270, 1 SDD 75, 2 SDD, 1340, ARB Nos 20, 21; ROB, Nos 11, 12
62 CDD pp 19 21, 2 SDD 886, 889 890, BBB, Nos 12 15, 16 17
63 CDD pp 21, 22 2 SDD 890 BBB No 17
64 CDD, p 25 2 SDD 895 896 BBB Nos 24, 25
65 CDD pp 17, 18 2 SDD 884 885, BBB Nos 10 11
66 CDD pp 25 274 2 SDD 895 1349 BBB No 24 ROB No 22
67 CDD pp 167 169 170 272 273, 429 1 SDD 588, 589, 592 593, 2 SDD 1347 896 FYB, Nos 36 37, 41, 43, ROB, Nos 18, 19, GWB, Ex 13, (Scott No 15)

his government to leave the Russian government no room for doubt that Austria in the event of a conflict with Russia would not stand alone" Austria was therefore at this time certain that Germany had already instructed her ambassador at St Petersburg to let it be known that she would stand by Austria[68]

The *German* chancellor said later "We were perfectly aware that a possible warlike attitude of Austria against Servia, might bring Russia upon the field and might therefore involve us in a war, in accordance with our duties as allies"[69]

Pretended surprise at Russia's interest

Yet under these circumstances the *Austrian* Minister for Foreign Affairs telegraphed his ambassadors at St Petersburg, London, Paris, and Rome, that he had just handed to the German ambassador at Vienna the statement that Austria "cannot conceal their astonishment that their action against Servia was directed against Russia and Russian influence in the Balkans"[70]

Russia's position

Russia's views as expressed to the British Ambassador at St Petersburg were "Austria's action was in reality directed against Russia She aimed at overthrowing the present *status quo* in the Balkans, and establishing her own hegemony there He (the Russian Minister for Foreign Affairs), did not believe Germany really wanted war, but her attitude was decided by" England's It England took a "stand firmly with France and Russia, there would be no war" It England "failed them now, rivers of blood would flow," and she "would in the end be dragged into war"

England not bound by alliance

The *British* Ambassador replied "that England could play the role of mediator at Berlin and Vienna to better purpose as friend who, if her counsels of moderation were disregarded might one day be converted into an ally, than if she were to declare herself Russia's ally at once His Excellency said that unfortunately Germany was convinced that she could count on" England's neutrality

The British Ambassador also said all he "could to impress prudence on the Minister for Foreign Affairs, and warned him that if Russia mobilized, Germany would not be content with mere mobilization, or give Russia time to carry out hers, but would probably declare war at once His Excellency replied that Russia could not allow Austria to crush Servia and become the predominant power in the Balkans and, if she feels secure of the support of France, she will face all the risks of war He assured me once more that he did not wish to precipitate a conflict, but that unless Germany could restrain Austria I could regard the situation as desperate"[71]

68 CDD, pp 3, 501 2 SDD, 864 1 SDD 81, BBB, No 3, ARB, No. 26
69 CDD, p 406, 2 SDD 771 GWB No 1
70 CDD, p 521 1 SDD 106, ARB No 44
71 CDD pp 21 22, 2 SDD 850 BBB, No 17

SERVIAN REPLY

Servia agrees to nearly everything

Servia put in her reply to Austria at 5 45 p m It was conciliatory in the extreme, it granted everything possible, while it did not admit official complicity in the propaganda and crimes charged, it promised immediate investigation and punishment of any found guilty, and removal of any such from office, it promised immediate dissolution and suppression of the alleged offending societies, although there was no proof submitted of their guilt, it promised so to amend the constitution and laws, by the legislative bodies then about to meet, that the means of propaganda by such societies and newspapers could be confiscated, as requested, it promised to suppress such propaganda in all public instruction, and while it was not clear as to exactly what was meant by the demand that Austrian officials should be permitted to participate in the investigations and measures of suppression, Servia would do all that her own laws, the rules of international law, and good neighborly acts would permit or require, Tankosic had already been arrested, a warrant had been issued for Ciganowic, but he had not yet been found, with these modifications it promised to make the publications in the official bulletins as requested, and if any of the matters were not satisfactorily answered, it proposed that they be submitted to the Hague Peace Tribunal, or to a conference of the Powers [73]

Austria's demand to supervise

Reply declared unsatisfactory

The *Austrian Ambassador* at Belgrade scarcely stopped to read the reply He declared it unsatisfactory, and within three quarters of an hour left Belgrade with the whole diplomatic outfit [74]

Austria's objections

Austria could make very little objection to its tone or contents, but declared it a sham and insincere, and later (July 25) sent to the other powers copies of the reply with her annotations and objections to each article of the reply, and a *dossier*, containing extensive quotations from alleged confessions, affidavits, and evidence obtained in the investigation made at Serajevo, to support her original charges, but which she had not furnished to Servia [75] She claimed that since peaceable means "were exhausted," she must "at last appeal to force," "in a fight that was forced" on her, "as a matter of self-defense," and "the Servians had refused the one thing—the co-operation of Austrian

---

72 Grey said it "went farther than could have been expected" "involved the greatest humiliation to Servia" that he "had ever seen a country undergo," and if Austria did not accept it but "marched into Servia it meant that she was determined to crush Servia at all costs" CDD pp 41, 43 281 2 SDD 916, 918 1379 BBB Nos 46 48, ROB No 42 Russia thought "it exceeded all our expectations in its moderation," and could not see how Austria could ask more "unless the Vienna Cabinet is seeking for a pretext for a war with Servia" CDD 278 2 SDD 1355, ROB No 37

73 CDD, pp 31 390, 417, 501 2 SDD, 904, 1477, 787, BBB, No 39, SBB, No 41 GWB Tel etc ARB, Nos 34 24

74 CDD pp 24, 390, 391, 273 279 2 SDD, 895, 1476, 1477 1348, 1356, BBB, No 23, SBB Nos 40, 41, 42, ROB, Nos 21, 37

75 CDD pp 193 197 461 1 SDD 29 637, 641 FYB, Nos 75 (2), 80 CDD pp 417, 507, 2 SDD, 785 1 SDD, 88, GWB Tel, etc, ARB, Nos 34, 19

officials and police—which would be a real guarantee that in practice the Servians would not carry on their subversive campaign against Austria"[76] Explanation was to be made at St Petersburg, "in strict confidence with regard to point 5—the participation of Austrian officials in the subversive movement in Servia—that "this clause was interpolated merely out of practical considerations, and was in no way intended to infringe on the sovereignty of Servia"[77]

German officials maintained that "Servian concessions were all a sham," and "The Servian Note, therefore is entirely a play for time"[78] The reply was not printed in Germany, in full, until after July 28, nor in Austria, apparently, and was received in France after twenty hours delay, and about the same, in Russia[79] — Germany takes time — Delay in publishing

Military preparations began at once Servia issued an order for immediate mobilization, Austria claiming this was done at 3 o'clock, about three hours before the Servian reply was put in[80] On the other hand, as early as July 11, at Budapest cannon and ammunition were being sent by Austria to the Servian frontier,[81] on the 20th military preparations were being made "in the vicinity of the Servian frontier"[82] On the 22 and 23, "eight army corps" were said "to be ready to start on the campaign",[83] on the 25th Austria said Servia could still "bring about friendly solution by unconditional acceptance of our demands" but she would have to reimburse "all costs and damage incurred by us through our military measures,"[84] indicating that she had already taken military steps, probably the mobilization of the eight corps On the 26th Austria certainly began mobilization, at least in part[85] Germany began clearing of trees, placing armament, constructing batteries, and strengthening wire entanglements on the French frontier[86] This was before France had begun[87] Russia authorized the mobilization of thirteen army corps, to be used if Austria brought armed pressure on Servia, but only after further notice was given by the Minister of Foreign Affairs, and on the 26th, "not a single horse and not a single reservist had been called up" — Servia — Austria — Germany — France — Russia

76 CDD, p 41, 2 SDD, 918, BBB No 48 (Communicated July 27, to Grey) As to self-defense, it should be remembered that Austria had 52,000,000 population, and Servia, 4,500,000 However about half of the population of Austria-Hungary is of Slavic descent, with more or less of Servian sympathies dominated by about 22,000,000 Germans and Magyars

77 CDD, p 503, 1 SDD, 83 ARB No 27

78 CDD, pp 29 123 2 SDD, 901 BBB No 32 GWB Tel, etc

79 CDD, pp 282 193, 506 178, 270, 1 SDD, 637, 88, 607, 2 SDD, 1361, 1340, ROB, Nos 46 13 FYB Nos 75 (2) 56

80 CDD pp 391 500 29 2 SDD 1477, 1 SDD 76, 2 SDD 900 SBB, No 41, ARB, No 23 BBB No 22

81 CDD p 116, 1 SDD, 558, FYB No 11

82 CDD p 388 2 SDD, 1463, SBB No 31

83 CDD, pp 150, 152 1 SDD 564, 566 FYB, Nos 18 20

84 CDD, p 499, 1 SDD 75 ARB, No 20

85 CDD, 181, 1 SDD 609, FYB, No 57

86 CDD p 215, 1 SDD, 663, FYB No 106 CDD p 223, 1 SDD 674 FYB No 118

87 CDD, pp 174, 503, 1 SDD, 602 84 FYB, No 70 ARB, No 28

but only "measures of preparation in the military districts of Kioff, Odessa and perhaps Kasan and Moscow" had been taken

Sunday, July 26, 1914

Russia requests Austria to exchange views

Russia asked Austria to exchange private views with her with the object of changing some of the demands of the ultimatum[88] No answer being received promptly, she then asked Germany to advise or request Austria to do this[89] This however was not done, and Austria declined Russia's request two days later[90]

Denied

French and German intercession

The *German* ambassador asked France to intercede with Russia, claiming that "the prevention of war depends on the decision of Russia' France replied "that Russia was moderate,' there was "no doubt as to her moderation,' and "Germany ought to act at Vienna, where her action would certainly be effective, with a view to avoiding military operations leading to the occupation of Servia" He refused,—"this could not be reconciled with the position taken up by Germany 'that the question concerned only Austria and Servia'"[91]

England requests conference of powers

England asked France Italy, and Germany to meet in London to confer in order to preserve the peace[92] France,[93] and Italy[94] immediately agreed to this Russia also immediately agreed to this, "or any other proposal of a kind that would bring about a favorable solution of the conflict," if her own "direct conversations, already urged with Austria were denied"[95]

Germany refuses

Germany at once refused,—this "would practically amount to a court of arbitration and could not be called together except at the request of Austria and Russia,'"[96] and it was in vain that it was explained the plan "had nothing to do with arbitration but meant that representatives of the four nations not directly interested should discuss and suggest means for avoiding a dangerous situation'

Kaiser returns

The *Kaiser*, "to the regret' of the German Foreign Office, suddenly returned on his own initiative, to Berlin, from Norway, where he had gone about three weeks before, ostensibly for his health[97] It was feared "that His Majesty's sudden return may cause speculation and excitement

—

88 CDD, pp 39, 40, 47 177 275, 2 SDD 914 916, 925, 1350, 1 SDD, 606 BBB Nos 43, 47 47 FYB No 54, ROB No 25
89 CDD, p 275 2 SDD 1351, ROB, No 26
90 CDD, pp 58 517, 2 SDD 939, 1 SDD, 101 BBB No 74, ARB, No 30
91 CDD, pp 179 181 1 SDD 607, 609, FYB, Nos 56, 57
92 CDD, pp 30 38 42 45, 47 52 2 SDD, 902, 913 918, 920 924, 925 931 BBB Nos 36, 42 43 49 52 53 60
93 CDD, pp 38, 47, 2 SDD, 913, 924, BBB, Nos 42, 52
94 CDD, p 43 2 SDD, 920 BBB No 49
95 CDD, pp 47, 49, 2 SDD, 925 927, BBB, Nos 53, 55.
96 CDD pp 38 52 515, 2 SDD 914, 931, 1 SDD, 98, BBB, Nos 43, 60 61, 62 ARB No 35
97 CDD p 29, 2 SDD, 901 BBB No 33, Beck Ev in Case, p 103

Monday, July 27, 1914

Powers request no invasion

France urged that England, France, Germany, and Italy again request Servia and Austria not to invade each other's territory, but that more time be given for negotiations.[98] Germany immediately refused, "because that would be to set up a real conference to deal with the affairs of Austria and Russia" and she "could not consent to anything" of the kind.[99] It had already been explained that this assumed "specter of a conference," and "mediation," meant no such thing as Germany urged but only "friendly advice," "peaceful words," or "friendly conversations."[100]

Germany refuses to join

Germany asked to urge direct conversations

Russia asked Germany to urge,—"to press with greater insistence"—Austria to accept Russia's suggestion of direct conversations with her "to draw up, by means of a private exchange of views," such "a wording of the Austro-Hungarian demands" as "would be acceptable to both parties."[101] The German Secretary of State offered to telegraph to the German ambassador at Vienna "in this sense," but refused "to advise Austria to give way." On the next day Austria answered she "could no longer recede, nor enter into any discussion about the terms of the Austro-Hungarian note."[102] The Austrian Under Secretary of State informed the Russian ambassador at Vienna, that a skirmish had already taken place on the Danube, begun by *the Servians*.[103] *The Russian ambassador then offered to do "all he could to keep the Servians quiet* pending any discussions that might yet take place" and would advise his government to urge Servia "to avoid any conflict as long as possible, and to fall back before an Austrian advance." The Secretary promised to "submit this suggestion to the Minister for Foreign Affairs."[104] Nothing came of it.

Austria refuses

Russia offers to restrain Servia

Servia's alleged invasion of Austria

As just stated *Austria* claimed that acts of aggression had occurred by Servian troops firing on Austrian troops "on the Danube" and "on the frontier," and this was alleged as one of the excuses for declaring war the next day, and refusing England's proposals for preventing "the outbreak of hostilities."[105] It is difficult to believe that little Servia should deliberately begin an attack on big Austria, just at a time when she knew all her friends were making every effort to prevent war.

German secretary not yet read Servian reply

The *German* Secretary of State said "he was obliged to keep his

---

98 CDD pp 183, 188, 189, 280, 1 SDD, 612, 618, 619, 2 SDD 1357, FYB, Nos 61, 68, 70, ROB, No 39

99 CDD pp 190, 191, 280, 1 SDD, 622, 2 SDD, 1357 FYB, Nos 73, 74, ROB, No 39

100 CDD, pp 72 181, 189 278, 1 SDD, 609, 619, 2 SDD 931 1354, BBB No 62, FYB Nos 59, 70, ROB, No 34

101 CDD, p 279, 2 SDD 1356, ROB No 38

102 CDD p 70, 2 SDD, 954, BBB, No 93 (1)

103 CDD, p 50, 2 SDD 928, BBB No 56

104 CDD, p 50, 2 SDD 928 BBB No 56

105 CDD, pp 50 518, 519, 2 SDD, 928, 1 SDD, 102, 103, BBB, No 56, ARB, Nos 40 41

engagements towards Austria," although he had "not yet had time" to read the Servian reply which he had received that morning. The French ambassador entreated him "in the name of humanity to weigh the terms in" his conscience and not to assume a part of the responsibility for the catastrophe which he was "allowing to be prepared."[106]

Germany's claim of mediation

The German Chancellor told England that "we have at once started the mediation proposal in Vienna in the sense as desired by Sir Edward Grey," and communicated Russia's desire "for a direct parley with Vienna," and that Austria answers "that after the opening of hostilities by Servia and the subsequent declaration of war, the step appears belated."[107] The published records of neither Germany nor Austria disclose how or when mediation was started by Germany, nor how urgent it was nor why it became "belated,"—since war was not declared till the next day.

Tuesday, July 28, 1914

Austria again refuses to discuss

Although yesterday *Russia* told Austria that she "was not prepared to give way again as she had * * * during the annexation crisis of 1909,"[108] *Austria* declared "that no discussion could be accepted on basis of Servian note, war would be declared today, (28th), the well-known pacific character of the Emperor, might be accepted as a guarantee that war was both just and inevitable," and "Russia ought not to oppose operations like those impending, which did not aim at territorial aggrandizement, and which could no longer be postponed."[109] The German ambassador at Paris stated "that Austria would respect the integrity of Servia," but as to "whether her independence also would be respected, he gave no assurance."[110] Russia "would not be satisfied with any engagement which Austria might make on these two points" if she attacked Servia,[111] and Sir Edward Grey thought it would be quite possible "without nominally interfering with the independence of Servia or taking away any of her territory to turn her into a sort of a vassal state."[112]

War declared on Servia

War was then declared at noon this day against Servia by Austria, and her army mobilized,[113] if it had not been before.

Summary of various efforts to preserve peace

Up to this point five concrete proposals for peace,—a joint request by all the powers, except Germany, for an extension of the time for the Servian reply,—Russia's request for a modification of some of the

---

106 CDD p 191 1 SDD 622 FYB No 74
107 CDD, 429, 430, 2 SDD, 806, 807, GWB, Nos 14, 15, 16, (Scott, Nos 16 17 18)
108 CDD p 50, 2 SDD, 928 BBB No 56
109 CDD p 52 2 SDD 931 BBB No 62
110 CDD, p 51, 2 SDD 930, BBB, No 59
111 CDD p 57, 2 SDD 937, BBB No 72
112 CDD, p 69 2 SDD 953 BBB No 91
113 CDD pp 43 51 54, 515; 2 SDD, 920, 930, 934, 1 SDD 99, BBB, Nos 70 59 66 ARB, No 37

Austrian demands, by a direct exchange of views between herself and Austria,—England's request that frontiers be not crossed by Austria or Servia until time was allowed for further consideration,—England and France's request that conversations by the disinterested powers, including Germany, take place at Vienna and St Petersburg,—and England's proposal for a joint conference of the same powers at London,—had been made, all coming from England, France, or Russia, and all agreed to by them, but all had been rejected or delayed by Austria and Germany [114]

The *Kaiser* now took a hand At 10 45 p m he telegraphed the Czar of Russia to this effect "The unscrupulous agitation which has been going on for years in Servia' led to the murder, this spirit still dominates that country, all sovereigns have a common interest to see deserved punishment inflicted "I shall use my entire influence to induce Austria Hungary to obtain a frank and satisfactory understanding with Russia"[115] Kaiser takes part

Wednesday, July 29, 1914

The *German* ambassador informed Russia "in the name of the Chancellor, that Germany has not ceased to exercise a moderating influence at Vienna, and that she will continue to do so even after the declaration of war"[116] What this "moderating influence" was is not revealed by the text of any document made public by Germany or Austria The Chancellor told the British ambassador at Berlin 'that events had marched too rapidly to act' on England's "suggestion that the Servian reply might form the basis of discussion", that on receiving the Servian reply he had "despatched a message to Vienna, in which he explained that, although a certain desire had, in his opinion been shown in the Servian reply to meet the demands of Austria he understood entirely that, without some sure guarantees that Servia would carry out in their entirety the demands made on her,' Austria "could not rest satisfied in view of their past experience', "that the hostilities which were about to be undertaken against Servia, had presumably the exclusive object of securing such guarantees" since Austria had "already assured" Russia "that they had no territorial designs" "He advised" Austria, "should this view be correct, to speak openly in this sense' and "such language would, he hoped eliminate all possible misunderstandings," and "since he had gone so far in giving advice at Vienna" he hoped England "would realize that he was sincerely doing all in his power to prevent danger of Germany's position

114 See Sazonof SDD p 101, 2 SDD 991 BBB No 139
115 CDD, p. 431, 2 SDD, 808, (No 22-I) GWB, No 20
116 CDD, p 71, 2 SDD, 955, BBB, No 93 (2).

European complications, and "doing his best to support" England's "efforts in the cause of general peace"[117]

Danger of exciting Austria

The same day the German Secretary of State reminded the British ambassador at Berlin, that he had said "the other day that he had to be very careful of giving advice to Austria as any idea that they were being pressed would be likely to cause them to precipitate matters and present a *fait accompli* This had, in fact, now happened, and he was not sure that his communication of England's "suggestion that Servia's reply offered a basis for discussion had not hastened declaration of war by Austria"[118] Truly German "mediation and advice" were not effective

Germany threatens Russia if she mobilizes

This same day too, "The German ambassador came to tell M Sazonof, (Russian Minister for Foreign Affairs), that if Russia does not stop her military preparations the German army will receive the order to mobilize" Sazonof replied that Russia's mobilization was caused by the "uncompromising attitude of Austria" and "that eight Austro-Hungarian army corps are already mobilized"[119] Sazonof also explained to the German ambassador that none of these military measures "were directed against Germany, neither should they be taken as aggressive measures against Austria-Hungary their explanation being the mobilization of the greater part of the Austro-Hungarian army"[120]

Russia decides to mobilize

The *French* ambassador at St Petersburg says "The tone in which" the German ambassador "delivered this communication has decided Russia this very night to order the mobilization of thirteen army corps which are to operate against Austria"[121] The German ambassador must have acted with authority and if so, German *mediation* at Vienna took the shape of *threats* at St Petersburg, as requested by Austria the day before, to tell Russia—"in a friendly manner," that, —although Russia has given her word of honor that up to then mobilization had not been ordered, but would be in "the military districts which border on Austria-Hungary—Kieff, Odessa, Moscow, and Kasan," if the Austrian troops "cross the Servian frontier,"—"should these measures be carried out, they would be answered by the most extensive counter measures, not only by the Monarchy but by our Ally, the German Empire"[122]

Russia's proposal to discuss refused

Russia had the same day, apparently before she knew Austria had declared war, suggested that both direct discussions, and the plans for a conference of the four powers continue,[123] but after Austria refused the further direct exchange of views with Russia, Sazonof said

---

117 CDD, p 58, 2 SDD, 939, BBB, No 75
118 CDD, p 59, 2 SDD 940, BBB No 76
119 CDD, p 210, 1 SDD 658, FYB, No 100
120 CDD, p 71 1 SDD 955 BBB, No 93 (2)
121 CDD, p 210, 1 SDD, 658, FYB, No 100
122 CDD, p 520 524, 1 SDD 104, ARB No 42 48
123 CDD, p 60 2 SDD, 941, BBB, No 78

that he would agree to any arrangement approved by France, England and Italy, or the four powers, "provided it was acceptable to Servia, he could not, he said, be more Servian than Servia," and indicated that if thought advisable, the Austrian ambassador might be called into the proposed conference

Russia favors conference

Germany objects to conference

The *German* ambassador at London told Sir Edward Grey that the German Chancellor was "endeavoring to mediate between Vienna and St Petersburg, and he hopes with good success" Sir Edward replied that Austria had declined this, but that the German government had before said "they were favorable in principle to mediation between Russia and Austria if necessary They seemed to think that the particular method of conference, consultation or discussion, or even conversations *a quatre* in London too formal a method" He then urged that the German Government should suggest *any method* by which the influence of the four Powers could be used together to prevent war between Austria and Russia France agreed, Italy agreed The whole idea of mediation or mediating influence was ready to be put in operation by *any method* that Germany could suggest * * * by any method that Germany thought possible if only Germany would 'press the button' in the interests of peace"[124]

The *French* Prime Minister, Viviani, told the German ambassador at Paris that if Germany wished for peace she should hasten to give her support to the British proposal for mediation, the ambassador said "the words 'conference' or 'arbitration' alarmed Austria "Viviani retorted that it was not a question of words and that it would be easy to find some other form for mediation" He added that "France sincerely desired peace, but that she was determined at the same time to act in complete harmony with her allies and friends"[125] The unsatisfactory answer to these suggestions of France and England is given tomorrow The German ambassador at Vienna was still feigning "surprise that the Servian affairs should be of such interest to Russia"[126]

Czar asks for help from Kaiser

The *Czar* of Russia, telegraphed the Kaiser at 1 p m, saying "I am glad you are back in Germany * * * I ask you to help me An ignominious war has been declared against a weak country, and in Russia the indignation which I fully share is tremendous I fear that very soon I shall be unable to resist the pressure exercised upon me and that I shall be forced to take measures which will lead to war * * * I urge you in the name of our old friendship to do all in your power to restrain your ally from going too far"[127]

---

124 CDD, p 63 2 SDD 946 BBB No 84 also, CDD pp 68 209 285, 2 SDD, 951 1366 1 SDD 656 BBB No 90, FYB, No 98, ROB, No 54

125 CDD p 286, 2 SDD 1366 ROB No 55

126 CDD, p 73, 2 SDD 958 BBB No 94

127 CDD, p 131, 2 SDD, 809 No 22 II GWB, No 21

Kaiser's reply—Russia to remain spectator while Austria goes on

Austria was then bombarding Belgrade, the capital of Servia.[128]

The *Kaiser* answered the Czar's telegram at 6 30 p m, saying "I share your desire for the conservation of peace * * * I cannot consider the action of" Austria "as an 'ignominious war'", it is "an attempt to receive full guaranty that the promises of Servia are effectively translated into deeds" Austria "intended no territorial gain at the expense of Servia" * * * It is perfectly possible for Russia to remain a spectator in the Austro-Servian war without drawing Europe into the most terrible war it has even seen" "I believe that a direct understanding is possible and desirable between" Russia and Austria, which "my government endeavors to aid with all possible effort" "Military measures by Russia which might be construed as a menace by" Austria "would accelerate a calamity which both of us desire to avoid and would undermine my position as mediator," which on your appeal for my aid "I willingly accepted"[129]

It should be noted that the Czar had asked the Kaiser's help to restrain his ally from going too far What, if anything, the Kaiser did in the line of this request, is not divulged in the published records, but what he did otherwise will soon appear

Czar asks explanation of Germany's threat

The *Czar* answered at 8 20 p m "Thanks for your telegram which is conciliatory and friendly, whereas the official message presented today by your ambassador to my minister was conveyed in a very different tone I beg you to explain this divergency It would be right to give over the Austro-Servian problem to The Hague Tribunal I trust in your wisdom and friendship"[130] (See the threat of German mobilization, by the German ambassador, above)

England would be involved

It should be noted that Sir Edward Grey today informed the German ambassador at London, that in case Germany and France became involved he "did not wish him to be misled into thinking that we should stand aside,"[131] and at the same time he told France not to be "misled into supposing that we had decided what to do" "in such a contingency"[132]

Thursday, July 30, 1914

Kaiser's answer, Russian mobilization interfere with mediation

The *Kaiser* answered the last telegram of the Czar, at 1 a m: Austria "has mobilized only against Servia, and only part of her army. If Russia * * * mobilizes against" Austria, "the part of mediator with which you have entrusted me * * * and which I have accepted

128 Baldwin, The World War p 238 Beck, Evidence in the Case, p 113 (Archer, however says not till afternoon)
129 CDD p 431, 2 SDD 809 No 22 III, GWB, No 22
130 CDD p 542 2 SDD, 1029, (This telegram is not printed with the others given in the GWB)
131 CDD, pp 67, 78, 2 SDD 950, 965 BBB, Nos 89, 102.
132 CDD, p 65 2 SDD, 948, BBB, No 87.

upon your express desire, is threatened if not impossible * * * You have to bear the responsibility for war or peace"[133]

At 2 a m the German ambassador at St Petersburg, "completely broke down on seeing that war was inevitable" "appealed to Sazonof to make some suggestion which he could telegraph to the German government as a last hope"[134]. Sazonof replied "The Emperor Nicholas is so anxious to prevent war that I am going to make a new proposal to you in his name" 'If Austria, recognizing that her dispute with Servia has assumed the character of a question of European interest, declares herself ready to eliminate from her ultimatum the clauses which are damaging to the sovereignty of Servia, Russia undertakes to stop all military preparations'"[135] This was sent to Berlin at once, and answered by the German Secretary of State, (Von Jagow), "that he considered it impossible for Austria to accept"[136] or "he found this proposal unacceptable to Austria"[137] "Mediation" by Germany had again failed At this moment news of proclamation of general mobilization by Austria reached St Petersburg,[137a] although it seems not to have been declared till 1 a m the next morning[137b]

Russia makes another proposition

Germany turns this down

As to *England, France, and Italy's* request of yesterday that Germany suggest *any method* of preserving peace,—the German Secretary of State "to draw up himself the formula for the intervention of the disinterested powers,"—the Secretary of State said "that to gain time, he had decided to act directly, and that he had asked Austria to tell him the ground on which conversations might be opened with her,"[138] "and was still awaiting to hear from her ally"[139] "No answer had, however, yet been returned" The Chancellor said "he was 'pressing the button' as hard as he could, and that he was not sure whether he had not gone so far in urging moderation at Vienna that matters had been precipitated rather than otherwise"[140] Again the language in which moderation was urged, and the manner of 'pressing the button' are withheld, but the French ambassador at Vienna, had word from Berlin, that the German ambassador at Vienna "is instructed to speak seriously" to Austria, "against acting in the manner calculated to provoke European war," but unfortunately he "is himself so identified with extreme anti-Russian and anti-Servian

Powers request Germany to suggest any method

Referred to Vienna

Germany "pressing the button"

133 CDD p 432, 2 SDD, 810, No 22, V GWB No 23
134 CDD, p 75 2 SDD 960, BBB No 97
135 CDD, p 212, 1 SDD 660 FYB No 103 See also CDD pp 75, 91, 288 291, 2 SDD, 960, 965 981, 1369, 1373, BBB, Nos 97, 103 120, ROB Nos 60, 67
136 CDD, 280, 2 SDD, 1371, ROB No 63
137 CDD p 216, 1 SDD 664 FYB No 107
137a CDD, p 297, 2 SDD, 1378, ROB, No 77 See CDD, p 216, 1 SDD, 664, FYB No 107
137b CDD, pp 222, 1 SDD, 672, FYB No 115
138 CDD, p 216, 1 SDD 666, FYB No 109
139 CDD, p 215 1 SDD 664, FYB No 107
140 CDD p 84 2 SDD 972 BBB, No 107

feeling in Vienna that he is unlikely to plead the cause of peace with entire sincerity."[140a]

Czar's answer again urges Kaiser to put pressure on Austria

The *Czar* answered the Kaiser's morning telegram, at 1 20 p m, saying "The military measures now taking form were decided upon five days ago, and for the reason of defence against the preparations of Austria I hope * * * these measures will not influence in any manner your position as mediator * * * We need your strong pressure upon Austria so that an understanding can be arrived at with us."[141] It will be noted that the Kaiser's telegram of 6 30 the night before took the position that Russia should remain a spectator, while Austria crushed Servia "in the Austro-Servian war", but the Czar was asking him to put pressure on to restrain his ally from going too far, as he had promised to do in his telegram of the 28th, and which presaged so well (Unfortunately there is no record of what, if any effort was made by the Kaiser in this direction It is difficult to believe he would not have been successful if he had made any real effort)

Germany asks England to induce France and Russia to remain neutral

Prince Henry of Prussia telegraphed King George of England telling him of Russia's military preparations, and "that France is making military preparations while we have not taken measures of any kind, but may be obliged to do so at any moment if our neighbors continue their preparations This would then mean a European war," and proposed that he should use his "influence on France and also on Russia that they should remain neutral * * * I consider this a certain and, perhaps, the only way of maintaining the peace of Europe."[142] This telegram had the approval of the Kaiser There is no indication of any pressure being put on Austria She was still to be left free to crush Servia

140a CDD, p 71 2 SDD, 959, BBB No 95

(a) NOTE—Mr Archer (Thirteen Days p 131), and Mr Headlam (Twelve Days, p 239), give a copy of a telegram dated today July 30, and printed in the Westminster Gazette of August 1 purporting to have been sent by the German Chancellor to the German ambassador at Vienna, saying "We cannot expect Austria to negotiate with Servia with which she is at war The refusal however to exchange views with St Petersburg would be a grave mistake We are ready to fulfill our duty as an ally We must, however refuse to be drawn into a world conflagration through Austria not respecting our advice Your excellency will express this to Count Berchtold with all emphasis and great seriousness" This telegram is not printed in either the GWB or the ARB Because the French ambassador heard of this proposed "serious" talk on the same day, Mr Archer thinks there is some probability of the telegram being genuine if it is genuine, it is the only bit of evidence that has come to light in which, the actual words in which Germany put any pressure on Austria, are given If it accomplished anything, it did no more than induce Austria to open up negotiations with Russia—only to be overthrown immediately by the Kaiser's demobilizing ultimatum It is very doubtful, to me, if it was genuine, or that it had the effect supposed, in view of the record, given in the text, relating to the Kaiser's telegram of 2 o'clock of this day It seems to me that a more obvious explanation of this belated, unofficially published, telegram is that it was invented and published at a critical time, for English consumption, instead of for Austrian action

141 CDD p 432 2 SDD 810 No 22, VI, GWB, No 23a

142 CDD p 538 2 SDD, 1023

King George suggests Austria hold Belgrade as a pledge

King George answered That England was "doing the utmost possible in order to induce Russia and France to postpone further military preparations provided that Austria declares herself satisfied with the occupation of Belgrade and the neighboring Servian territory as a pledge for a satisfactory settlement of her demands, while at the same time the other countries suspend their preparations for war I rely on William applying his great influence in order to induce Austria to accept this proposal"[143] It seems that the suggestion that Austria hold Belgrade as a pledge was made July 29, by Sir Edward Grey to the German ambassador at London who, today (30th) said the "German government would endeavor to influence Austria after taking Belgrade and Servian territory in region of frontier, to promise not to advance further while Powers endeavored to arrange that Servia should give satisfaction sufficient to pacify Austria Territory would of course be evacuated when Austria was satisfied"[144] The German Secretary of State says "he asked Austro-Hungarian government whether they would be willing to accept mediation" on this basis, but "has up till now received no reply" and "fears Russian mobilization against Austria will have increased difficulties, as Austria, who has as yet only mobilized against Servia, will probably find it necessary also against Russia," and if Russia will agree "to above basis" and "take no steps which might be regarded as an act of aggression against Austria," there is some chance to preserve peace"[145] The German Chancellor says "he had begged Austria to reply to" this proposal and "had received a reply to the effect that Austrian Minister for Foreign Affairs would take wishes of the Emperor this morning"[146]

Germany agrees to influence Austria

No reply

Referred to Austrian Emperor

Yesterday the *Russian* ambassador at Vienna had requested that direct conversations between Sazonof and the Austrian ambassador at St Petersburg be resumed, but his request was "flatly refused"[147] Today, however, "it was agreed that *pourparlers* should be resumed" not to modify the Austrian ultimatum to Servia, but only "to discuss what settlement would be compatible with the dignity and prestige" of Russia and Austria This revived hope, to be dispelled instantly, for just then "news of the German mobilization arrived in Vienna"[148] (It is claimed that this was a mistake, and is considered below) The instructions given to the Austrian ambassador at St Petersburg for carrying on the discussion were to make "any explanation he desired with regard to the note—which in any case appears to be outstripped by the outbreak of war, * * * it was never intended to depart in

Discussions to be renewed

But not to change demands

143 CDD p 538, 2 SDD, 1021
144 CDD p 78, 2 SDD 965 BBB No 103
145 CDD, p 75, 2 SDD 961 BBB No 98
146 CDD p 87, 2 SDD 975 BBB No 112
147 CDD p 205 1 SDD 652 FYB No 93
148 CDD, p 213, 1 SDD, 662, FYB No 101

any way from the points contained in the note" It was stated in these instructions that Austria "had mobilized exclusively against Servia, against Russia, not a single man."[149] although in the earlier conversation mobilization in Galicia (which would be toward Russia) was admitted, but stated to "have no aggressive intention and" is only to maintain "the situation as it stands"[150]

German military activities

France reported that Germany had recalled "the reservists by tens of thousands", "officers of reserve have been summoned", "the German army has its outposts on our frontier, the whole 16th army corps from Metz, reinforced by part of the 8th from Treves and Cologne, occupies the frontier from Metz to Luxemburg, the 15th army corps from Strassburg is massed on the frontier" And "although Germany has made her covering dispositions a few hundred meters from the frontier along the whole front from Luxemburg to the Vosges, and has transported her covering troops to their war positions, we have kept our troops ten kilometers (6 miles) from the frontier and forbidden them to approach nearer" "On two occasions yesterday (29th) German patrols penetrated our territory"[151]

ENGLAND'S NEUTRALITY

England refuses to join France and Russia

This, perhaps, is a good place to say something more about England's neutrality,—"perfidious Albion" As we saw above, (July 25), England was urged from the first to stand solidly with Russia and France,—otherwise Germany and Austria would count on her neutrality,—but refused on the ground that she could mediate with them better as a friend, than as an ally of Russia[152] On July 24, she postponed the demobilization of her First Fleet, assembled a few days before at Portland for review On the 27th this was made public,[153] and the Russian ambassador at London was told it meant nothing more "than diplomatic action was promised"[154] On the same day the German ambassador was informed by Grey "that our fleet was to have dispersed today, but we had felt unable to let it do so, "there was no menace in what we had done, but owing to the possibility of an European conflagration, it was impossible for us to disperse our forces at the moment"[155]

Germany warned England would not stand aside

As we saw above, yesterday afternoon, (29th), Grey warned the German ambassador at London that Germany could not count on England's neutrality if all efforts to preserve peace failed[156] The German

149 CDD, p 525, 1 SDD, 111, ARB, No 50
150 CDD, p 213, 1 SDD, 662, FYB No 104
151 CDD, pp 76 214, 2 SDD, 962, 1 SDD, 663; BBB No 99, FYB, No 106
152 CDD, pp 14 22 39, 2 SDD 880 890 915, BBB, Nos 6, 17, 44
153 CDD, p 187, 1 SDD 617, FYB, No 66
154 CDD p 41, 2 SDD 917 BBB, No 47
155 CDD p 43 2 SDD, 918 BBB, No 48
156 CDD pp 67 65 2 SDD, 930 948, BBB, Nos 89, 87

ambassador sent a telegram to that effect, which reached Berlin late that night [157] Before it is said to have been delivered the German Chancellor who "had just returned from Potsdam," invited the British ambassador to call on him that evening He said, 'should Austria be attacked by Russia a European conflagration might become inevitable owing to Germany's obligation as Austria's ally,' and made "the following strong bid for British neutrality," saying that "so far as he was able to judge * * * Great Britain would never stand by and allow France to be crushed, * * * that was not the object at which Germany aimed,' if the "neutrality of Great Britain were certain every assurance would be given to" England that Germany "aimed at no territorial acquisition at the expense of France should" Germany be "victorious in any war that might ensue" When asked "about the French colonies, he said he was unable to give a similar undertaking" but would respect the territory of Holland and Belgium if her adversaries did the same The British ambassador answered at once that he did not think England would bind herself, but would "desire to retain full liberty" [158] Sir Edward Grey answered this "bid," today (30th), this way England "cannot for a moment entertain the Chancellor's proposal" to bind herself "to neutrality on such terms What he asks us in effect is to engage to stand by while French colonies are taken and France is beaten so long as Germany does not take French territory' in Europe "Such a proposal is unacceptable, for France * * could be so crushed as to lose her position as a great Power, and become subordinate to German policy, it would be a disgrace for us to make this bargain with Germany at the expense of France, a disgrace from which the good name of this country would never recover' The Chancellor also asks us to bargain away our interest in the neutrality of Belgium "We could not entertain that bargain either' [159]

Germany bid for English neutrality

England refuses to be bound

Today also the *German* ambassador asked "why Great Britain was taking military measures both on land and sea' and was told 'that these measures had no aggressive character but the situation was such that each power must be ready' [160]

English mobilization

Friday, July 31, 1914

At 1 a m today Austria declared mobilization for all men between 19 and 42 years of age [161]

The *Russian* ambassador at Vienna reported that Austria is determined not to yield to intervention of powers and was moving troops

Russia will not yield

157 CDD, pp 78, 76 2 SDD, 965 961 BBB, Nos 102 98
158 CDD, p 64, 2 SDD, 947, BBB, No 87
159 CDD, p 77 2 SDD 964 BBB, No 101
160 CDD p 290 2 SDD 1372 ROB No 65
161 CDD, p 222 1 SDD 672 FYB, No 115

against Russia, as well as against Servia Russia then ordered general mobilization,[162] early in the day

Russia's and England's proposals fail

Russia's proposition to stop military preparations if Austria would recognize the European character of the Servian question, and allow some modification of the terms of the ultimatum, (which the German Secretary of State, yesterday refused to forward to Austria), and England's proposition that Austria hold Belgrade as a pledge, and stop further military advances, (referred to the Austrian Emperor to be answered this morning), were amalgamated into one to the effect If Austria will agree to check her advance on Servian territory recognize the dispute is of European interest, and allow the powers to determine whether Servia can satisfy Austria without impairing her independence and sovereignty, Russia will maintain her waiting attitude[163] This was sent to Vienna at once, but neither it nor the original proposition seems to have received any consideration[164]

Germany requested to urge mediation

On the 29th *England* urged Germany to propose some method by which the four powers could work together to preserve peace, but Russia insisted that Austria suspend military operations against Servia in the meantime, otherwise mediation would drag on and give Austria time to crush Servia Sir Edward Grey, however, thought that mediation might still be possible, even after Belgrade was seized, if Austria would advance no further, "pending an effort of powers to mediate *between her and Russia*, and that it "was more important than ever that Germany should take up" this matter with Austria[165] This seems to have been sent through Germany *the next day to Austria*,[166] and reply sent today, (31st), by Austria, but not received till August 1, at London and St Petersburg, to this effect "We are quite prepared to entertain the proposal of Sir E Grey to negotiate *between us and Servia* The conditions are * * * that our military action against Servia should continue to take its course" and England should induce Russia to bring to a standstill her mobilization against us, and we will cancel our defensive military countermeasures in Galicia[167] Again German mediation had only had the effect that Austria persisted in her demand that she be allowed a free hand to crush Servia, while negotiations went on

Further proposals by England

Today Sir Edward Grey made two further proposals to Germany 1 That if Germany would sound Austria, he would sound St Petersburg, as to whether it would not be possible for the four powers to

162 CDD p 87, 2 SDD, 976, BBB, No 113 Also CDD, p 527, 1 SDD, 113, ARB, No 52

163 CDD p 91 291 2 SDD 981 1373, BBB No 120, ROB, No 67, CDD pp 219, 220 1 SDD 669 670 FYB, Nos 112, 113

164 CDD p 102 2 SDD 991, BBB, No 139

165 CDD, p 66 2 SDD 949, BBB No 88

166 CDD p 75 2 SDD 961 BBB No 98

167. CDD p 526 1 SDD, 112, ARB, No 51

guarantee Austria full satisfaction against Servia, without impairing her sovereignty and integrity, on the one hand and on the other, guaranteeing to Russia that Servia's sovereignty and integrity, should not be impaired, by Austria And 2, he said "If Germany could get any reasonable proposal put forward which made it clear that Germany and Austria were striving to preserve European peace, and that Russia and France would be unreasonable if they rejected it" he "would support it at St Petersburg and at Paris," and if they would not accept it England "would have nothing more to do with the consequences" The only answer was that "it was impossible for" Germany "to consider any proposal until they had received an answer from Russia to their" ultimatum to demobilize immediately, sent that day and referred to below [168]

Yet, for some reason not clearly disclosed by the record, *Austria* today suddenly faced about, and agreed to renew discussions,—and "far from harboring any designs against the integrity of Servia, was in fact ready to discuss the grounds of her grievances against Servia with the other Powers ." [169] "to discuss with Russia" and "to accept a basis of mediation which is not open to the objection to the formula which Russia originally suggested ", [170] "to discuss the substance of the Austrian ultimatum to Servia" [171] Austria then knew that Russia had ordered general mobilization early in the day, [172] and had herself taken military measures in Galicia, but these had no aggressive intention and were not to stop *pourparlers* between Russia and Austria, and from which she hoped "things will quiet down all round" [173]

Austria agrees to discuss

Russia immediately accepted this offer suggested "that the discussions should take place in London with the participation of the Great Powers," and hoped England "would assume the direction of these discussions" "It would be very important that Austria should meanwhile put a stop provisionally to her military action on Servian territory" but this was not made a condition of Russia's acceptance [174] Here seemed to be a wide open opportunity for discussion and mediation, with every chance of settlement,—but war "is the game that kings play at"

The *Czar* telegraphed the Kaiser, as to Russian military preparations, which had been so strenuously objected to "It is technically impossible to discontinue our military preparations which have been made necessary by the Austrian mobilization * * * As long as the negotiations between Austria and Servia continue, my troops will undertake no provocative action I give you my solemn word there-

Czar's telegram about Russia's military preparations

168 CDD, pp 86 92 2 SDD 974 982 BBB Nos 111, 121
169 CDD p 293, 2 SDD, 1375 ROB, No 73
170 CDD p 97 2 SDD 988 BBB No 131
171 CDD, p 97 2 SDD 989 BBB No 133
172 CDD, p 527 1 SDD, 113 ARB No 52
173 CDD p 527 1 SDD 113 ARB No 53
174 CDD, p 98, 2 SDD, 989 BBB No 133

on[175] This assumes Austria had agreed to reopen negotiations, (as she had), and although she had not agreed to stop her military measures, Russia was willing to give assurance that *her* troops would take no action

aiser's legram out Russia's obilization

This telegram of the Czar was crossed by one to the Czar, sent at 2 p m by the *Kaiser*, mainly scolding him for mobilizing against Austria, "my ally," whereby "my mediation has become almost illusory," but saying further "I receive reliable news that serious preparations for war are going on on my eastern frontier The responsibility for the security of my country forces me to measures of defence" * * * "No one threatens the honor and peace of Russia which might well have awaited the success of my mediation" * "the peace of Europe can still be preserved by you if Russia decides to discontinue those military preparations which menace Germany and Austria-Hungary"[176] It is clear that since Austria had already agreed to negotiate further, of which the Czar already had knowledge, Austria's change was not due to the Kaiser's "mediation," or the Kaiser was ignorant of his own success, up to 2 o'clock, or prevaricated I cannot believe he was ignorant Neither can I believe his Chancellor and Secretary of State were ignorant of Austria's agreement to negotiate further,—although the latter, late this evening, declared that the Kaiser and the Foreign Office "had even up to last night been urging Austria to show willingness to continue discussions,—but Russian mobilization had spoilt everything"[177] This last statement was untrue, for Austria knew Russia had issued order for general mobilization before she agreed to negotiate further,[178] and the claim of the German Secretary of State, made the next day, "that Austria's readiness to discuss was the result of German influence at Vienna," was false[179]

ermany's timatum to ussia

Notwithstanding this agreement of Austria, and notwithstanding that "so long as conversation with Austria continued" the Czar "undertook that not a single man should be moved across the frontier,"—all of which must have been known to the Kaiser and his Chancellor,—they sent an ultimatum to Russia, at midnight that night, July 31, to be answered within 12 hours, that is by noon, Saturday, demanding that Russia immediately demobilize her whole army, against both Austria, and Germany,—"if Russia does not stop every measure of war against us and against Austria-Hungary within 12 hours, and notifies us definitely to this effect," mobilization of the German army is bound to follow, "although we have up to this hour made no preparations for mobilization, Russia has mobilized her entire army

175 CDD, p 411, 2 SDD, 778, GWB Statement Aug 3d
176 CDD, p 411 2 SDD, 778, GWB, Statement Aug 3d
177 CDD, p 92 2 SDD, 982, BBB, No 121
178 CDD, p 527, 1 SDD 113 ABB Nos 52 53
179 CDD, p 100, 2 SDD 993, BBB, No 138

and navy, hence also against us," and we have thereby "been forced for the safety of the country to proclaim the threatening state of war, (*Kriegsgefahrzustand*) which does not yet imply mobilization"[180]

Austria had mobilized at 1 a m, Russia, "early in the day," "as a result of the general mobilization of Austria and of the measures for mobilization taken secretly, but continuously, by Germany for the last six days,"[181] as reported by the French ambassador at St Petersburg, in contradiction of the German Chancellor's statement above. The "state of danger of war," (*Kriegsgefahrzustand war-danger-state*) is admittedly a German technical term, which after being proclaimed, according to the Chancellor, "Mobilization would follow almost immediately",[182] and according to the German ambassador's statement to the French Minister for Foreign Affairs, the publication of this was impending as early as the 29th, "and under the protection of this screen," after its publication at mid-day today, (31st),[183] Germany "immediately began mobilization in the proper sense of the word"[184] **Mobilization by Germany**

The *German* Chancellor's telegram above to Russia, to demobilize within 12 hours, says that "we have up to this hour made no preparations for mobilization" "At the same time the Imperial (German) ambassador in Paris was instructed to demand from the French Government a declaration within 18 hours whether it would remain neutral in a Russo-German war"[185] The text of the telegram sent to France, (as it appears in the German text of the German White Book), also says "we ourselves have taken no measures towards mobilization" However, the German "only authorized translation" into English, leaves out this statement

Since Germany's ultimata to Russia and France, are specifically based on her alleged knowledge of Russia's order for general mobilization, and Russia's order was itself based on the alleged mobilization of Austria and Germany, it is necessary to look into these matters a little more There is no important difference, as between Austria and Russia,—both understood they were mobilizing against one another, but not with aggressive purposes, while the discussions were going on as agreed As between Germany and Russia, the documents show much uncertainty

When Germany *sent* her "demobilizing ultimatum" to Russia, she undoubtedly had knowledge of Russia's order of mobilization, the hour when the telegram was sent is not given, it however was delivered at midnight,[186] the one sent to France, "at the same time,"

---

180 CDD p 433 2 SDD 811 No 23 GWB Ex 24
181 CDD p 223 1 SDD 671, FYB No 118
182 CDD p 86 2 SDD 975 BBB No 112
183 CDD, p 222, 1 SDD, 673, FYB, No 117
184 CDD, p 231, 1 SDD 681, FYB No 127
185 CDD p 412, 2 SDD, 779, GWB, Statement Aug 3
186 CDD, p 412, 2 SDD 779, GWB, Statement Aug 3

and marked with "utmost speed," was delivered at 7 p m [187] The Kaiser said in his telegram to King George, sent in the evening, that his Chancellor had just heard that "Nicholas this *evening* has ordered the mobilization of his entire army and fleet" *Evening*, in Germany, means from 5 to 10 p m In the Kaiser's telegram above, sent at 2 p m, he complains of Russia's *mobilization* against his ally, Austria, not against Germany, but only of "reliable news of serious preparations for war going on on my eastern front" If he had then had knowledge of the mobilization of Russia's "entire army and navy, hence also against us, he would have said so, yet the German authorized English text, (for use in England), of the statement made August 3d by the German Foreign Office, (after war was declared with Russia) says "the mobilization of all the Russian forces obviously directed against us and already ordered in the *afternoon* was in full swing Notwithstanding the telegram of the Czar was sent at 2 o'clock that same afternoon" The German text of the same document (for use in Germany), says that Russia mobilized in the *morning* [188] It seems a reasonable inference that Germany first learned of Russia's *mobilization* in the *evening*, (after 5 p m), instead of *afternoon* (2 p m), or in the *morning*, as stated in the juggled documents Is there any reason for this juggling? Let us consider

Germany's ultimatum to Russia to *demobilize*, also said that Russia's mobilization was the cause of Germany's declaring her "state of danger of war," (*Kriegsgefahrzustand* literally, *war-danger-state*), also This was decided on at *mid-day* that day,[189] at least two hours before the German authorized English text of the statement of August 3d, says Russia had mobilized, and several hours before the Kaiser knew of it in the *evening*, for German use at least it therefore would be necessary to allege that Russia's mobilization was known in Germany in the *morning* otherwise Germany's declaration of a "state of danger of war," *could not* be based on the reasons claimed

It has come to light since that the German proclamation decided on at mid-day instead of announcing a "state of danger of war," (*Kriegsgefahrzustand*), as told to England, France and Russia, actually proclaimed a "state of war," (*Kriegszustand,—war-state*),—(*das Reichsgebiet* *wird hierdurch in Kriegszustand erklart*) [190] Just before 2 o'clock a director of the North German Lloyd, sent to Berlin to ascertain conditions, telegraphed his board, "that the declaration of a state of war (*Kriegszustand*), would at once be made public and later in the day notified them of "the declaration of the

187 CDD pp 88, 222 327, 2 SDD, 978, 1 SDD, 673, 114, BBB No. 117 FYB No 117, ARB No 54
188 CDD, p 412 2 SDD 779 GWB Statement, Aug 3
189 CDD, p 222 1 SDD 673 FYB No 117
190 Wilson H W, New Light on Germany's Treachery, Nineteenth Century, June, 1917, pp 1204 1214

state of war for the German Empire, owing to the threatening danger of war,'—again not giving Russian *mobilization* as the reason, but only the threatening danger of war[191] Now, the difference between *Kriegsgefahrzustand* (*war-danger-state*), and *Kriegszustand* (*war state*), is important, for the German mobilization cards held by German soldiers, direct them automatically to report at once to their headquarters, "upon the existence of a 'state of war,'" but not on the existence of a "state of danger of war" So that by this trick of proclaiming a "state of war" at mid day, July 31, instead of "a state of danger of war" as reported to the other governments, they were misled, and the German soldiers called to their posts

But *Russia* mobilized because she understood Germany was secretly doing so Did she have any substantial reason to think so? Russian and German mobilization

In the evening of July 29, an Extraordinary Council was held at Potsdam with the military authorities, under the presidency of the Kaiser, and decided on mobilization, and probably on the invasion of Belgium About 1 o'clock p m, July 30, the *Lokal Anzeiger*, a semi-official newspaper, in a special edition, published news of the mobilization of the German army and fleet[192] This was immediately telegraphed to Russia,[193]—18 to 20 hours before Russian mobilization was ordered News of the German mobilization was received in Vienna at about the same time[194]

At 2 o'clock p m, the German Secretary of State, telephoned the French and Russian ambassadors at Berlin, that "the news of mobilization of the German army and fleet, which has just been announced, is false, that the news sheets had been printed in advance so as to be ready for all eventualities, and that they were put on sale in the afternoon, but that they now have been confiscated"[195] The English and Austrian ambassadors do not seem to have been so notified The French ambassador at Berlin said he believed "that all the measures for mobilization which can be taken before the general order of mobilization have already been taken here, and that they are anxious here to make us publish our mobilization first, in order to attribute the responsibility to us"[196] The same reasons and remarks would equally apply to Russia

It has since been learned that the Berlin correspondent for a Vienna newspaper, at 10 o clock a m, July 30, telegraphed his paper announcing that German mobilization had been proclaimed and that he had received this news "from one of the Emperor's staff So too, it now appears that four other Berlin newspapers besides the

191 The Kronprinzessin (1916) 228 Fed Rep 94, 951
192 CDD, p 213 1 SDD, 662, FYB No 105
193 CDD, p 289, 2 SDD 1370 ROB No 61
194 CDD, 213, 1 SDD 661, FYB No 104
195 CDD p 289, 2 SDD 1370, ROB, No 62
196 CDD, p 214, 1 SDD 662, FYB No 105

Lokal Anzeiger, at the same time published special editions announcing mobilization by Germany It is difficult to believe that all of these could suddenly have conceived such an idea at the same time as to special editions, unless they had been authoritatively so informed [197] On the same day the 20th French army corps at Nancy intercepted a telephone message between Metz and Strassburg, saying that mobilization began that evening After the German Secretary of State said this publication was false, the Russian ambassador at Berlin so notified his home government, as above given

Other facts however make it certain that what was substantially equivalent to mobilization[198] was going on in Germany from July 21, when it was secretly begun by Germany's peculiar preliminary notice [199] On the 23d, German officers on leave in Basle were ordered to return to Germany [200] On the 24th, the colonels of the German regiments at Metz, began giving their officers instructions as to the duties of covering troops, only given immediately before mobilization On the 25th railway stations in Germany were filled with soldiers in uniform, and for the next two days movement by trains of cavalry, artillery, and infantry toward the Belgian frontier was begun We have already noted above the German activities on the French frontier on this date On the 26th, the German fleet in Norway was ordered to return to Germany [201] Reservists were directed to hold themselves at the disposition of the *Kommandatur* at any moment [202] On the 27th motor car owners in Baden were secretly notified (under penalty of fine) to hold their cars at the disposal of the military authorities within two days after call [203] Men on leave were ordered to rejoin their regiments, five classes of reservists, (1,250,000 men), were called, these with the peace strength, (over 800,000 men), made more than 2,000,000 men, German officers at Antwerp were secretly directed to report to their regiments, German troops began to deploy on the Luxemburg frontier On the 28th and 29th uniformed troops were passing through Frankfort from Darmstadt, Cassel and Mayence, which were full of soldiers, and bridges

197 Wilson, H W, New Light on Germany's Treachery, Nineteenth Century June 1917, pp 1204-1214

198 "Careful usage distinguishes between" *military preparations* and *mobilization*, "though it is hard to draw the line" *Mobilization* means to make mobile making ready to move, bringing together men, materials and all other military paraphernalia for instant use in war such as filling up the regiments of the first line to full war strength by recalling men on furlough, summoning reservists and forming them into second and third lines, corresponding to the first line, taking over railways, and collecting and equipping all the machinery of transportation and communication,—telegraphs, telephones motor cars horses vehicles ships, etc, for army service, gathering, forwarding and providing for the distribution of arms, ammunition, uniforms food supply etc, necessary before beginning to move to various places of assembly to be from there *deployed* in battle array

199 CDD pp 134 149 1 SDD, 544 562 FYB, Nos 3 17

200 CDD, p 182, 1 SDD, 612, FYB, No 60

201 CDD, p 182, 1 SDD 612, FYB, No 58

202 CDD p 182, 1 SDD 611 FYB, No 59

203 CDD, p 182, 1 SDD, 612, FYB, No 60

and railways were guarded, under pretext of preparation for autumn manoeuvers,[204] mills in Alsace were directed to stop deliveries to clients and hold supplies for the army, at Strassburg motor-guns were going forward non-commissioned officers of Bavarian infantry regiments at Metz, in Bavaria on harvest leave received orders to return immediately, under *pretext of change in autumn manoeuvers*[205] Hamburg American and North German Lloyd steamers were directed to embark reservists On the 29th the whole German covering force were at their posts on the French frontier. 30 military trains passed between Metz and Treves and the 18th army corps was concentrated at Frankfurt In Bavaria and Wurtemburg army corps were marching west The *Ersatz* reservists,—(1,500,000 men), received notices which automatically called them up on the proclamation of a state of war This was the condition of things when the War Council met that evening We have already noted the German military activities on the French frontier on the 30th By that time an army of more than 3,500,000 men was practically mobilized by Germany Yet the Chancellor, about 5 p m, July 31, telegraphs Russia saying "we have up to this hour made no preparations for mobilization'"[207] On the other hand Sazonof said on the 30th, "that absolute proof was in the possession of Russian Government that Germany was making military and naval preparations against Russia—more particularly in the direction of the Gulf of Finland"[206] Which was probably correct?[208]

But without any reference as to who mobilized *first*, the Kaiser, after knowing that Austria had expressed a willingness to negotiate with Russia, or with all the Powers, and after he had the Czar's promise on his honor that his army would take no action as long as negotiations continued, sent this ultimatum to Russia, to be answered within 12 hours demanding that she *demobilize* her whole army, against both Austria and Germany, and without any promise or suggestion that he or Austria would do the same The reason why demobilization against Austria as well as against Germany was demanded, was, as stated by the Secretary of State, Von Jagow, "in order to prevent Russia from saying all her mobilization was only directed against Austria "[209]

Kaiser's responsibility.

---

204 CDD, p 202, SDD 648 FYB No 88
205 CDD, p 202 1 SDD 649 FYB No 89
206 CDD p 431 2 SDD 811 No 23, GWB No 24
207 CDD, p 75, 2 SDD, 960 BBB No 97
208 The facts concerning mobilization by Germany above given for which no specific reference is given, are from Wilson's article in the Nineteenth Century for June 1917 New Light on Germany's Treachery, pp 1201-1214
209 CDD, p 92, 2 SDD 982 BBB No 121

Saturday, August 1, 1914

Czar asks for guarantee from Kaiser

The *Czar* answered the Kaiser, (not within the 12 hour limit, but at 2 o'clock), saying "I comprehend that you are forced to mobilize, but I should like to have from you the same guaranty which I have given you, viz, that these measures do not mean war and that we shall continue to negotiate for the welfare of our two countries, and the universal peace which is so dear to our hearts "[210]

Refused to consider

The *Kaiser* answered "I have shown yesterday to your government the way (that is, by immediate demobilization) through which alone war may yet be averted Although I asked for a reply by today noon, no telegram from my ambassador has reached me with the reply of your government I therefore have been forced to mobilize my army An immediate and unmistakable reply of your government is the sole way to avoid endless misery Until I receive this reply I am unable, to my great grief, to enter upon the subject of your telegram "[211]

Germany declares war on Russia

At 12 52 p m the German Chancellor notified the German ambassador at St Petersburg that "If the Russian Government gives no satisfactory reply to our demand," you "will please transmit this afternoon 5 o'clock (mid-European time), the following * * * Russia having refused to comply with this demand, and having shown by this refusal that her action was directed against Germany * * * I have the honor * * * to inform your Excellency as follows —His Majesty the Emperor, my august Sovereign, in the name of the German Empire accepts the challenge, and considers himself at war with Russia "[212] This was delivered at 7 10 p m[213]

England urges Germany to stay her hand

England again urged that since Austria and Russia were willing to discuss matters, and it "Germany did not want war on her own account" she "should hold her hand and continue to work for a peaceful settlement " The Secretary of State replied that "Austria's readiness to discuss was the result of German influence at Vienna, and, had not Russia mobilized all would have been well But Russia by abstaining from answering Germany's demand that she should demobilize, had caused Germany to mobilize also Russia had said that her mobilization did not necessarily imply war, and that she could perfectly well remain mobilized for months without making war This was not the case with Germany She had the speed and Russia had the numbers, and the safety of the German Empire forbade that Germany should allow Russia time to bring up masses of troops from all parts of her wide dominions "[214]

210 CDD, p 413 2 SDD 770 GWB, Statement Aug 3
211 CDD 413 2 SDD, 770 GWB Statement Aug 3
212 CDD, pp 294 433, 2 SDD 1377 S11, No 25, ROB, No 76, GWB, No 26
213 Same references
214 CDD, p 100 2 SDD 993, BBB, No 138

According to the statement of the *German* Foreign office to the German people August 3, 1914, in the afternoon of August 1, before the delivery of the order declaring war "Russian troops crossed our frontier and marched into German territory. Thus Russia began war against us."[215] This same document also says "As the time limit given to Russia had expired without the receipt of a reply to our inquiry, H. M., the Kaiser ordered the mobilization of the entire German army and navy on August 1, at 5 p. m." In the document declaring war Russian *mobilization*, not Russian *invasion* is given as the cause of the declaration of war.

Germany claims Russia invaded her

Germany has constantly claimed that she did not mobilize until August 1, at 5 p. m., Saturday, and after Russia had mobilized against her and had invaded her territory, and her war was therefore, one of defence only, as claimed in the Kaiser's speech referred to in the early part of this paper. As to *invasion* of Germany by Russia, this is inherently improbable, Russia did not want war with Germany, she and Austria were about to discuss, instead of fight, although she had given orders to mobilize before Germany claims to have given her order, yet Germany had the speed, and Russia the numbers when she got them together, but since she certainly had not yet accomplished this why should she attack Germany before she was ready? Besides, the Czar had given his word of honor to the Kaiser that not a man should cross the line while negotiations continued. We have already discussed what Germany had been doing in the way of mobilizing for the past 15 days.

Germany claims war was defensive one

As to these matters of invasion and mobilization it is well to remember a few bits of history. As we have seen the Triple Alliance, is one of defense, and not of offense. Austria and Italy were bound by it to stand by Germany only in case she were attacked by Russia. So, too, by the constitution of the German Empire, the Kaiser has no right to declare an offensive war, but only a defensive one.[216] As we have seen, this war was declared by the Kaiser, and not by the Bundesrat, it had to be made a *defensive* one therefore. At the beginning of the Franco-Prussian war in 1870, it was said that "On July 19, at noon, a body of French soldiers crossed the Prussian frontier at Saarbrucken, and were driven back by the Uhlans. This was the first hostile act committed before the formal declaration of war." Subsequent histories make no mention of this. It had a special purpose to subserve then. Bavaria was then bound only by a *defensive* alliance to Prussia, and was wavering in her support, in the discussions in her legislative body, when this "act of hostility" was re-

Triple Alliance and defensive war

Constitution and offensive war

Similar conditions Franco-Prussian war

215 CDD p. 413. 2 SDD 780. GWB, Statement August 3.
216 "For a declaration of war in the name of the Empire the consent of the Bundesrat is required, unless an attack is made upon the federal territory or its coasts."—IV, Art. 11, Dodd, Modern Constitutions, Vol. 1, p. 331.

ported at the proper time, and with the desired result[217] So, here, Austria declared war on Russia, (August 6th), because she "has seen fit to open hostilities against Germany"[218] On August 1, however, Italy declared that this war was not a defensive one, but an aggressive war on the part of Austria, and she was not obliged under the terms of the Triple Alliance to take part in it[219] Just as in the beginning of the Franco-Prussian war hostile acts of France were counted on as above noted, so when Germany declared war on France, at 6 45 p m, August 3, 1914, she claimed France was guilty of "a certain number of flagrantly hostile acts committed on German territory," specifying "yesterday morning (August 2,) *eighty* French officers in Prussian uniform had attempted to cross the German frontier in *twelve* motor cars at Walbeck", and French military aviators have "attempted to destroy buildings near Wesel," and "thrown bombs on the railway near Carlsruhe, and Nuremburg" Now the 80 French officers in their 12 motor cars, would not only have to cross Belgium, but also 30 miles of Holland, to reach Walbeck, it is strange that they were seen by no one but Germans in their violation of the neutral territory of Belgium and Holland, on their 140 mile trip, and have not been heard from since, so, too, Wesel, is 150 miles from the French frontier, 30 of which is also across Holland, Carlsruhe is 85 miles from France, and Nuremburg 200, these early aviators have made no report,—they seem still to be in the air The German officer in command at Nuremburg has publicly denied that any bombing of the railway at that time occurred, and when the German government delivered her ultimatum to Belgium, August 2, she did not, and could not, allege any violation of Belgian territory by France, but only that she had "reliable information' of "the intention of France to march through Belgian territory against Germany" With these claims in mind, which were so far from the truth, the allegation that Russia began the war against Germany, does not carry much weight It and the rest of them served their purpose, just as Bismarck's "modified" Ems telegram in 1870 did

The Kaiser, therefore, with full knowledge of the willingness of Austria and Russia to negotiate further, with the assurance that Russia would take no military action while the negotiations continued and would stop military preparations if he would do the same, deliberately refused, declared war, and blocked all possibility of peace

And this is "How Russia and her ruler betrayed Germany's confidence and thereby made the European war'

---

217 Wilson, H W New Light on Germany's Treachery, Nineteenth Century June, 1917 pp 1204-1214

218 CDD, pp 298 529, 2 SDD, 1381 1 SDD, 117, FYB, No 79, ARB, No 59

219 CDD, pp 106, 228, 2 SDD 1002 1 SDD 679, BBB, No 152 FYB, No 124

Sunday, August 2, 1914

German troops violated French territory in at least 11 different places,—at one, Jonchery, six miles from the frontier, Lieutenant Mayer of the 5th mounted Jagers, of the 14th army corps blew out the brains of a French corporal, and was himself killed and two German troopers were taken prisoner,[220] also invaded Luxemburg, and Germany demanded that permission be given by Belgium to Germany for her troops to cross Belgian territory to invade France — *Invasion of France*

INVASION OF BELGIUM

By the settlement at the Congress of Vienna, in 1815, Holland and Belgium were joined together under the name of The Netherlands This was not a happy union, and in 1830, Belgium declared her independence of Holland Great Britain, Austria, France, Prussia, and Russia, by *treaty with her in 1831* recognized her independence "as a perpetually neutral state" and "guaranteed perpetual neutrality" Holland then objected, but in 1839, joined these powers in a treaty by which Belgium was to "form an independent and perpetually neutral state" placed "under the guarantee of" these powers—this guarantee being considered from the beginning to be 'to uphold, not collectively but severally and individually, the integrity of the treaty,' and not jointly as in the treaty of 1867, concerning the neutrality of Luxemburg [221] — *Neutrality of Belgium* — *Treaties*

By *treaty of 1870* during the Franco-Prussian war, Prussia, (practically on behalf of the North German Confederation, with which France was technically at war), declared her intention "to respect the neutrality of Belgium, so long as the same shall be respected by France" and England agreed to cooperate with Prussia in case France violated that neutrality This treaty between Prussia and England was to last during the continuance of the war and for 12 months after the ratification of peace, but "without impairing or invalidating the conditions of" the treaty of 1839, being only "subsidiary and accessory to it" A precisely similar treaty was entered into by England and France at the same time

In 1911, the *German* Chancellor had declared to Belgium "that — *Confirmations*

---

220 CDD pp 234 236, 1 SDD 686, 687, 689 FYB Nos 136 139 The German Chancellor says this was against express orders, GWB, Speech Aug 4, CDD, p 438

221 Mowat R B Select Treaties, Oxford Pamphlets, Introduction, and pp 37 42 Arts 9 and 10 of Treaty of 1831, and Art 7 of Treaty of 1839

222 Mowat Select Treaties p 39 Prof Burgess, argues that Germany is not a party to either of these treaties, since they were not made with either her or the North German Confederation He also says that Germany was not a party to the Hague Convention of 1907 As to this last he is mistaken as to the first, the original treaty of 1839 was made with his Majesty the '*King of Prussia*,' the present Kaiser, is still King of Prussia, and by virtue of this is Emperor of Germany Besides the German Chancellor did not think of such a flimsy excuse

Germany had no intention of violating Belgian neutrality," in 1913, the German Secretary of State had publically declared to the Budget Commission of the Reichstag, that "Belgian neutrality is provided for by International Conventions, and Germany is determined to respect those conventions" On July 31, 1914, the German Minister to Belgium, upon specific inquiry, told the Belgian Minister for Foreign Affairs, that he knew of these declarations of the Chancellor and Secretary of State, and "the sentiments expressed at that time had not changed" And again on August 2, (the day that Germany later in the day delivered her ultimatum to Belgium), the German Minister to Belgium confirmed "the feelings of security" which Belgium "had the right to entertain towards" her "eastern neighbors"[223]

Belgium's duty of self defense

By *the treaty of 1839*, Belgium was bound to do all she could, to defend her own neutrality, in case it was threatened or invaded The Hague Conference, 1907, declared the territory of neutral powers is inviolable, and belligerents are forbidden to move troops across it, and resistence is not an hostile act[224] Germany had signed this declaration

July 24 1914, *Belgium* mobilized her small army, and put her forts in a state of defense, and on the 29th "strengthened her peace footing" in order to perform her duty to protect her own neutrality[225]

France agrees to respect Belgian neutrality

July 31, the *French* Minister to Belgium, as soon as he learned of "the state of war in Germany" with Russia, immediately declared to the Belgian Foreign Minister, "that no incursion of French troops into Belgium will take place, even if considerable forces are massed upon the frontiers of your country" The same day *England* asked Belgium if she would "do her utmost to maintain her neutrality," and also asked France and Germany if they would respect Belgian neutrality, if violated by no other power[226]

France answered "Yes," at once, and on the same day so informed the Belgian Minister for Foreign Affairs[227] The *German* Secretary of State answered "that he must consult the Emperor and the Chancellor before he could possibly answer," and for fear of disclosing part "of their plan of campaign," he was "very doubtful whether they would return any answer at all"[228] The next day, Saturday, August 1, England insisted on an answer from Germany, saying "if there were a violation of the neutrality of Belgium by one combatant while the other

Germany does not

223 CDD, p 307 1 SDD 366, BGB No 12
224 Convention V, Chapter I, Articles 1, 2, 10 Germany's claims that Belgium had violated her duty of neutrality by understanding with England prior to the war are too flimsey to need comment
225 CDD, pp 300, 303, 1 SDD, 376, 364, BGB Nos 2, 8
226 CDD, pp 87, 307, 2 SDD 976 977, 1 SDD, 368, BBB, Nos 114, 115 BGB, No 13
227 CDD, pp 94, 227, 307; 2 SDD, 985, 1 SDD, 367, 369, BBB, No. 125 FYB, No 122 BGB No 15
228 CDD, pp 92, 227, 2 SDD 983, 1 SDD, 568; BBB, No 92, FYB, No 123

respected it, it would be extremely difficult to restrain public feeling in this country "[229] At 1 05 p m France answered Germany's ultimatum to her of the night before, "that France would do that which her interest dictated "[230] "The Kaiser ordered the mobilization of the entire German Army and Navy on August 1st at 5 p m," according to the Chancellor,—"the first day of mobilization to be 2d August," according to the newspaper reports[231] (But see above) France mobilized at 3 40 p m[232]

Germany sends ultimatum to Belgium demanding permission to march across to France

Sunday, August 2, at 7 p m *Germany* presented an ultimatum marked "very confidential" to Belgium, saying "Reliable information has been received by" Germany "that French forces intend to march * * * through Belgian territory against Germany," who fears "that Belgium * * * will be unable without assistance to repel so considerable a French invasion with sufficient prospect of success to * * * guarantee against danger to Germany It is essential for the self-defense of Germany that she should anticipate such hostile attack " And would regret "if Belgium regarded as an act of hostility" the "fact that the measures of Germany's opponents force Germany, for her own protection, to enter Belgian territory " If this was permitted Germany proposed "at the conclusion of peace to guarantee the possessions and independence of the Belgian Kingdom in full,' "to evacuate Belgian territory at the conclusion of peace , "to purchase all necessaries for her troops against a cash payment and to pay an indemnity for any damage that may have been caused by German troops " Should Belgium oppose * * * Germany will, to her regret, be compelled to consider Belgium as an enemy," and "the eventual adjustment of relations between the two states must be left to the decision of arms'[233] "A time limit of twelve hours was allowed in which to reply"[234] At 1 30 a m, the German Minister to Belgium, asked to see the Secretary General to the Belgian Minister for Foreign Affairs to tell him "he had been instructed by his Government to inform the Belgian Government that French dirigibles had thrown bombs, and a French cavalry patrol had crossed the frontier in violation of international law " When asked, Where? he replied, "in Germany " The Secretary then said "he could not understand the object of the communication,'—when the German Minister answered that "these acts, which were contrary to international law, were calculated to lead to the supposition that other acts, contrary to international law, would be com-

229 CDD p 93 2 SDD, 984 BBB, No 123
230 CDD, pp 434, 223, 2 SDD, 813, No 26, 1 SDD 673, GWB, Ex 26 FYB No 117
231 CDD pp 413 103 232 2 SDD, 780, 997, 1 SDD, 784, GWB, Statement Aug 3, BBB No 142 FYB No 130
232 CDD p 99 2 SDD, 991 BBB No 136
233 CDD pp 309 312 1 SDD 371 375, BGB, Nos 20 23
234 CDD, p 312 1 SDD, 375, BGB, No 23

mitted by France"[235] Six and a half hours earlier the German Government could only allege "we knew that France was ready to invade Belgium"[236] according to the Chancellor, and make that, "the lying pretext that Belgian neutrality was threatened by us,"[237] according to Viviani, as the basis of the ultimatum to Belgium

Belgium replies in negative

At 7 a m Monday, August 3, *Belgium replied*[238] "This note has made a deep and painful impression upon the Belgian Government The intentions attributed to France by Germany" contradict France's formal declarations, it "Belgian neutrality should be violated by France," Belgium "would offer the most vigorous resistance" "The treaties of 1839" and 1870, "vouch for the independence and neutrality of Belgium under the guarantee of the Powers" including Prussia "Belgium has always been faithful to her international obligations" "The attack upon her independence" which Germany threatens "constitutes a flagrant violation of international law No strategic interest justifies such a violation of law" If Belgium "were to accept the proposals submitted," she "would sacrifice the honor of the nation and betray" her "duty towards Europe," and she is "firmly resolved to repel, by all the means in" her power, "every attack upon" her rights " Caesar said more than nineteen hundred years ago, "Of all the Gauls, the Belgae are the bravest"[239]

France offers support

France immediately offered Belgium "the support of five French army corps," but she said she was "making no appeal at present to the guarantee of the powers"[240] At 6 45 p m, Germany declared war on France, because of the alleged acts of aggression above noted[241] Belgium appealed to England for diplomatic intervention on her behalf, and England immediately protested "against this violation of a treaty to which Germany is a party in common with" her, and requested an assurance from Germany that she would respect the neutrality of Belgium[242]

England warns Germany

On Tuesday, August 4, *England* told Belgium that if Germany applied pressure to induce her to depart from neutrality, she would expect her to resist by any means in her power, and she stood ready to join France and Russia "for the purpose of resisting use of force by Germany against" her[243]

Germany declares war on Belgium

At 6 a m, *Germany* declared war on Belgium, "in consequence of the refusal" by her "to entertain the

---

235 CDD, p 311, 1 SDD 372, BGB, No 21
236 CDD, p 317, 1 SDD 381 BGB No 35
237. CDD, p 259, 1 SDD 715, FYB No 159
238 CDD pp 311, 323 1 SDD 373, 389, BGB, Nos 22 44
239 The area of Belgium is 11,373 sq mi, population 7,500,000 Germany area, 208,000 sq mi population 67,000,000 In 1914 Belgium's war strength was 222,000 and Germany's 5,200,000
240 CDD, pp 106, 313 2 SDD, 1001, 1 SDD 375, BBB, No 151, BGB, No 24
241 CDD, pp 240 241, 1 SDD 693 694 FYB Nos 147, 148
242 CDD pp 107, 313, 2 SDD 1002 1 SDD 376, BBB, No 153, BGB, No 25
243 CDD, p 108, 2 SDD, 1003, BBB, No 155

well intentioned proposals' of Germany,[244] and immediately proceeded to invade her territory.[245]

The *reasons* given by the German Chancellor were: "We were in a state of legitimate defence, and necessity knows no law. Our troops have occupied Luxemburg and have perhaps already entered Belgium. This is contrary to * * * international law. France has * * * declared * * * that she was prepared to respect the neutrality of Belgium so long as it was respected by her adversary. But we knew that France was ready to invade Belgium. France could wait, we could not. A French attack upon our flank * * * might have been fatal. We were, therefore, compelled to ride roughshod over the legitimate protests' of Luxemburg and Belgium. "For the wrongs which we are thus doing, we will make reparation as soon as our military object is attained." "He who is menaced as we are and is fighting for his highest possession can only consider how he is to hack his way through."[246] The German Secretary of State gave as reasons that Germany "had to advance into France by the quickest and easiest way,"[247] and the Kaiser (in his suppressed cablegram to President Wilson, August 10, 1914), because of "strategical grounds, *news* having been received that France was already preparing to enter Belgium." (In the original, the word *knowledge* was crossed out, and *news* written instead.)[248] Reasons given—necessity

Belgium appealed "to Great Britain, France, and Russia to co-operate as guaranteeing powers in the defence of her territory."[249] Germany sent word to England that she "will, under no pretense whatever, annex Belgian territory", the "German army could not be exposed to French attack across Belgium, which was planned according to absolutely unimpeachable information."[250] Belgium appeals to powers

England again requested Germany to give assurances by midnight to respect the neutrality of Belgium, and proceed no further with their violation of "her frontier," and if not given then England would "feel bound to take all steps in" her "power to uphold the neutrality of Belgium and the observance of a treaty to which Germany is as much a party as" England.[251] England's ultimatum to Germany

That afternoon, the *German* Secretary of State answered "No," saying the German troops had crossed the frontier in the morning, and "Belgian neutrality had been already violated * * * the safety of Germany's answer—only "a scrap of paper"

244 CDD p 314, 1 SDD 377, BGB, No 27
245 CDD pp 109, 316, 321, 2 SDD, 1005, 1 SDD, 379 386, BBB No 158, BGB Nos 30 40
246 CDD pp 317, 438 1 SDD, 381 BGB No 35, GWB Appendix, Chancellor's Speech to the Reichstag, August 4 1914
247 CDD p 110, 2 SDD 1006 BBB, No 160
248 Ambassador Gerard's "My Four Years in Germany" p 438, Phil Public Ledger, Aug 5, 1917
249 CDD p 321, 1 SDD 386 BGB No 40
250 CDD, p 109 2 SDD 1004 BBB No 157
251 CDD, p 109, 110, 2 SDD 1005 BBB Nos 159 160

the Empire rendered it absolutely necessary that the Imperial troops should advance through Belgium" And that evening the Chancellor said that the step taken by England "was terrible to a degree, just for a word—'neutrality,' a word which in war time had so often been disregarded—just for a scrap of paper Great Britain was going to make war on a kindred nation who desired nothing better than to be friends with her'[252]

England's reply

England replied "for the honor of Great Britain, she should keep her solemn engagement to do her utmost to defend Belgium's neutrality if attacked,'[253] and "Germany, having rejected the British proposals" declared "that a state of war existed between the two countries as from 11 o'clock" that night[254]

ENGLAND'S RESPONSIBILITY

Germany first blames Russia

The statement of the *German* Foreign Office. August 3, 1914, says "Russia began the war against us," and the German Chancellor the next day said to the Reichstag, "Russia has set fire to the building We are at war with Russia and France,—a war that has been forced upon us"

Then England

In the Chancellor s speech, four months later, December 2, he declares that while the outer responsibility for the war is on Russia, the inner, lies upon England, for she gave Russia to understand that she placed herself at the side of Russia and France, she could have made it impossible, had she declared she would not suffer a European war to grow out of the Austro-Servian dispute, France would then have energetically warned Russia against military action, "then the way would have been clear for our mediatory action"

Russia's efforts to preserve peace

Russia s efforts toward peace have already been set forth in detail, from the first she declared she could not stand by and see Servia crushed, deprived of her integrity and independence, and become a vassal of Austria, she held to this throughout, yet in the beginning, (July 26) she told Austria that her claims were legitimate if she had no other aim than the protection of her territory against the intrigues of Servian anarchists, but her procedure was indefensible, and Sazanof said "Take back your ultimatum, modify its form, and I will guarantee you the result",[255] and at the end he accurately summed up his efforts, saying he "was completely weary of the ceaseless endeavors he had made to avoid war No suggestions held out to him had been refused He had accepted the proposal for a conference of four, for mediation by Great Britain and Italy, for direct conversations between Austria and Russia, but Germany and Austria-

---

252 CDD, pp 110, 111, 2 SDD, 1006, 1007, BBB, No 160
253 CDD, p 111, 2 SDD, 1007, BBB, No 160
254 CDD, p 322, 1 SDD, 387, BGB No 41
255 CDD p 177, 1 SDD 606 FYB, No 54

Hungary had either rendered these attempts for peace ineffective by evasive replies or had refused them altogther

France from the beginning told Russia that she would support her in negotiations, and as an ally in case of necessity, a course she adhered to throughout, yet supporting every effort toward peace made by any of the parties, counseling moderation at all times, and on the 29th July, at the critical time, inducing Russia to suspend for the time being every military measure that could offer Germany any pretext for general mobilization [257]

France's position

We have already seen above how, from the very first, (July 24), *England*, although strongly urged, refused to make any engagement to support Russia and France by force of arms [258] On July 27 Russia and Germany were informed that while the conflict continued between Austria and Servia alone, British interests were only indirectly affected, but Austrian mobilization might lead to Russian mobilization, then the interests of all the powers would be involved, in which case England "reserved to herself full liberty of action," and refused then to bring "conciliatory pressure" on Russia, at Germany's request [259]

England's position

On the 27th, the German and Austrian ambassadors in London allowed it to be understood that they were sure England would remain neutral if a conflict broke out,[260] but the German ambassador was immediately informed otherwise [261] On the 29th Sir Edward Grey made still clearer England's position to France and Germany He told the French ambassador that in a "Balkan quarrel, and in a struggle for supremacy between Teuton and Slav we should not feel called to intervene, should other issues be raised, and Germany and France became involved, so that the questions became one of the hegemony of Europe, we should then decide what it was necessary for us to do",[262] and to the German ambassador he said "There would be no question of our intervening if Germany was not involved, or even if France was not involved", but if British interests required us to intervene, we must intervene at once, and the decision would have to be very rapid [263] At the same time he told both that they should not be misled by these statements,—France into relying upon England's support, or Germany into thinking she would stand aside

Warns Germany early

We have already told how England declined Germany's bid for her neutrality, made this day, the 29th On the 30th the French Presi-

Refuses Germany's bid for neutrality

256 CDD, p 101, 2 SDD 994 BBB No 139
257 CDD, p 211, 1 SDD, 659, FYB, No 102
258 CDD, pp 14, 163, 2 SDD, 880, 1 SDD, 584, BBB, No 14, FYB, No 163
259 CDD, p 273, 2 SDD, 1348, ROB No 20
260 CDD, p 185, 1 SDD, 616, FYB No 63
261 CDD, p 43, 2 SDD 918 also CDD, p 41, 2 SDD 917, BBB, Nos 47, 48, also CDD p 282, 2 SDD, 1359, ROB No 42
262 CDD, p 65, 2 SDD 948, BBB, No 87
263 CDD, p 67, 2 SDD 950, BBB, No 89

dent again urged England to agree to come to her aid in case of a war between France and Germany, saying "there would then be no war, for Germany would at once modify her attitude," but England declined.[264] The next day in answer to a direct question by the German ambassador, whether Great Britain would remain neutral, he was told that if the conflict became general, and especially if France were involved, England would not be able to remain neutral, but would be brought in, at the same time France was informed that England could not then guarantee intervention on behalf of France, "but it was necessary to wait for the situation to develop."[265] Although England had several times refused to agree to stand solidly with Russia and France, Russia today thanked her for "the firm attitude" and "firm and friendly tone" adopted by her.[266] On the 2d of August, however, subject to the approval of Parliament Sir Edward Grey assured France that "if the German fleet comes into the Channel or through the North Sea to undertake hostile operations against French coasts or shipping, the British fleet will give all the protection in its power," but this "did not bind" England to go to war with Germany unless she took the action stated.[267]

Such is the Record of England, she gave neither Russia, France, nor Germany to understand that she placed herself at the side of Russia and France, the only way she could have made the war impossible, in the way the Chancellor stated, was to have told Russia and France that Austria and Germany were to have a free hand, under any circumstances.

Only in such a sense can England be said to be responsible, at least so far as Germany and Austria are concerned. But further as to the Chancellor's charge against England. The German documents themselves exonerate England from this charge. In the statement of the German Government sent to King George, August 1, 1914, that "The proposals made by the German Government at Vienna were conceived entirely on the lines suggested by Great Britain, and the German Government recommended them at Vienna for their serious consideration."[268] And the official statement of the German Foreign Office, August 3, 1914, says "Shoulder to shoulder with England we labored incessantly and supported every proposal in Vienna" offering the possibility of peace.[269] These relate to efforts claimed to have been made at *Vienna* and admit, by implication at least, none were made there by Germany except such as England suggested.

German Chancellor gave England credit

But as to Russia, the Chancellor himself says in his speech, August

264 CDD, p. 76, 2 SDD, 962, BBB, No. 99.
265 CDD, pp. 217, 543, 1 SDD, 667, 2 SDD, 1029, FYB, No. 110, Telegrams, etc., V. 1.
266 CDD, pp. 91, 291, 2 SDD, 981, 1374, BBB, No. 120, ROB, No. 69.
267 CDD, p. 105, 2 SDD, 999, BBB, No. 148.
268 CDD, p. 536, 2 SDD, 1020, Telegrams, etc., I. 1.
269 CDD, p. 410, 2 SDD, 777, GWB, Statement, Aug. 3.

4, 1914 "Great Britain, warmly supported by us, tried to mediate between Vienna and *St Petersburg* And the declaration of war by Germany against Russia August 1, says "the German Emperor had undertaken, *in concert with Great Britain* the part of mediator between the Cabinets of Vienna and *St Petersburg* Here again Great Britain's efforts at mediation with Russia, are admitted "Our (Germany's) mediatory action," therefore was not blocked, by England, either at Vienna or St Petersburg

But what of German mediation? That it was being continuously exercised, is constantly asserted, over and over again, by Kaiser, Chancellor, and Secretary of State So much so that "The lady doth protest too much, methinks" The terms of not a single peace proposal by Germany is divulged by the published records There is nothing but assertion, and demand of "localization," "no intervention," or "demobilization," under threat of mobilization by Austria or Germany, revealed by the documents, as the method of German mediation It was not only sterile of peaceful results, but had exactly the opposite effect Its absolute failure was attributed by Germany to the unapproachably haughty touchiness of Austria, or the "mobilization," or "invasion," by Servia, Russia, or France, bent on attacking their peace-loving neighbors, Austria and Germany German mediation

FACTS NOT IN THE RECORD

Such is the result of the published official records, with the few additional facts referred to in the notes There are, also, some other matters, not in the official records, yet fully established, that are necessary to complete the story Two of these are Further facts as to Germany's prior knowledge of the Servian ultimatum, and the Potsdam meeting Matters not in the record

As to the first Herr von Jagow, the German Secretary of State, on July 21st, before the ultimatum was delivered, told the Russian and French representatives at Berlin, "That he was in complete ignorance of the contents of that note"[270] The next day he repeated "he knew nothing of the text"[271] On the 24th, the day after the note was delivered to Servia, when asked by the French Ambassador at Berlin, "if the Berlin Cabinet had really been entirely ignorant of Austria's requirements before they were communicated to Belgrade," said, "that that was so"[272] On the 25th in answer to a similar inquiry by the English representative at Berlin, "he received so clear reply in the negative that he was not able to carry the matter further"[273] On the same day the German ambassador at London read Germany's hand in Austrian ultimatum

270 CDD p 149 1 SDD 562 FYB No 15
271 CDD, p 149 1 SDD 563 FYB No 17
272 CDD, p 161, 1 SDD 582 FYB No 30
273 CDD p 169, 1 SDD 592 FYB. No 41

a telegram to Sir Edward Grey, from the German Foreign Office saying "that his government had not known beforehand, and had had no more than other Powers to do with the stiff terms of the Austrian note to Servia."[274] England immediately sent this word to Russia.[275] At the same time the German ambassador at Paris said "that there had been no 'concert' between Austria and Germany in connection with the Austrian note, and that the German Government had no knowledge of this note when it was communicated to them at the same time as to the other Powers, though they had approved it subsequently."[276] And on this same day, 25th July, the German ambassador to Russia, handed a verbal note to the Russian Minister for Foreign Affairs, saying "We learn from an authoritative source that the news spread by certain newspapers to the effect that the action of Austria at Belgrade, was instigated by Germany, is absolutely false. The German Government had no knowledge of the text of the Austrian note before it was presented, and exercised no influence upon its contents. A threatening attitude is wrongly attributed to Germany."[277] July 26th, the German ambassador at Paris again "affirmed that Germany had been ignorant of the text of the Austrian note, and had only approved it after its delivery."[278] This was reiterated the 28th.[279] And finally in the Official Statement August 3, of the German Foreign Office, it is said "We guaranteed Austria a completely free hand, but have not participated in her preparations."[280]

Prior knowledge

On the other hand, on July 23d, the President of the Bavarian Council told the French Minister at Munich that "the contents of the Austrian note were known to him."[281] On the 24th Sazonof, the Russian Minister for Foreign Affairs declared that Austria "would never have taken such action unless Germany had first been consulted,"[282] and this was the universal belief, despite the German denials. On the 30th the British ambassador at Vienna reports that "Although I am not able to verify it, I have private information that the German Ambassador (here) knew the text of the ultimatum before it was despatched and telegraphed it to the German Emperor."[283] Such is what the record shows.

Von Jagow had knowledge

But since this was published *other facts* have become known. On September 3, 1916, Count Tisza, President of the Hungarian Ministry, in answer to the question if he had not talked over the Austrian note to Servia with German officials said: "I do not care to answer

---

274 CDD, p 25, 2 SDD, 896, BBB, No 25
275 CDD, p 273, 2 SDD, 1348, ROB No 20
276 CDD p 166, 1 SDD 588, FYB, No 36
277 CDD, p 272, 2 SDD, 1347, ROB, No 18
278 CDD p 181, 1 SDD 610, FYB, No 57
279 CDD, p 196, 1 SDD, 640, FYB, No 78
280 CDD, p 406, 2 SDD 773
281 CDD, p 153, 1 SDD 567, FYB No 21
282 CDD, p 14, 2 SDD 880, BBB No 6
283 CDD, p 74, 2 SDD 959, BBB No 95

that question directly But you can draw your own conclusions If a person has a very close and strong friend, and if he is about to take a step of the most terrible gravity, does he, or does he not, discuss the whole matter with his friend, and finally tell his friend what he has decided to do?" Three weeks later, Von Jagow, himself, the German Secretary of State when asked a question, based on what Tisza had divulged, said "I did not have a hand in preparing the note * * * I saw it at 8 o'clock the night before it was presented in Belgrade, where it was presented at 10 o'clock the next morning That was too late to do anything about it All we had done was to assure Austria that we would back her up in an attempt to punish Serbia"[284] (The note reached Belgrade at 10 o'clock, but was not actually delivered until 6 p m)

Again, July 14, eight days before the note was delivered, Baron Wangenheim, German ambassador at Constantinople, told the Italian ambassador there that "the Austrian note to Serbia would be such as to render war inevitable'"[285]

The Kaiser knew and approved

And again In the middle of July, 1914 Dr Muhlon then a director of Krupp's Works, at Essen, was told by Dr Helfferich, then a director of the Deutsche Bank, in Berlin, and later Vice-Chancellor of Germany, the following "The Austrians have just been with the Kaiser In a week's time Vienna will send a very severe ultimatum to Servia with a very short interval for the answer * * * The ultimatum will contain certain demands such as punishment of a number of officers, dissolution of political associations, criminal investigation by Austrian officials, and in fact a whole series of definite satisfactions will be demanded at once, otherwise Austria will declare war on Serbia, * * * the Kaiser expressed his decided approval of this procedure, and regarded a conflict with Serbia as an internal affair between these two countries, in which he would permit no other state to interfere If Russia mobilized, he would mobilize, and mobilization meant immediate war" When this was reported to Herr Krupp von Bohlen, he confirmed it and added, "the Kaiser had told him he would declare war immediately if Russia mobilized, and that this time people would see that he would not turn about * * * No one would be able to accuse him of indecision" On the day the Austrian ultimatum appeared Dr Helfferich told Dr Muhlon, "the Kaiser had gone on his northern cruise as a blind, but was remaining close at hand and keeping in close touch" The German Government's reply to Dr Muhlon's statement is that "the author is in a 'pathological state,' and consequently not responsible"[286]

---

284 W C Bullitt, interview with Tisza and Von Jagow, Phil. Pub Ledger, Aug 6, 1917

285 Speech of M Barzilai of the Italian Government, at Naples, Sept 24, 1915.—Facts about the War No 22 p 3

286 Facts about the War, No 82, May, 1918, Germany's Confession, U S Committee on Public Information

The Kaiser fixed the time limit

But still further Dr E J Dillon, Special Correspondent from south-eastern Europe for the London Daily Telegraph, and an authority on European Affairs, says as to the Austrian ultimatum "Nothing was kept back from the politicians of the Wilhelmstrasse but the rough draft of the note The German ambassador, von Tschirscky, however, was one of the few who were initiated into that mystery, * * * (he) saw the proposed text of the ultimatum, * * * it was he who telegraphed the wording of the document to the Kaiser * * * I advance this statement with a full knowledge of what actually took place This communication was made not merely for the purpose of keeping the War Lord informed, * * * but also to secure his express assent to exact terms of an official paper which was intended to bring about hostilities between Austria and Servia, and might * * * precipitate a European conflict, * * * the rough draft did not obtain (his) unconditional approval, (he) suggested a certain amendment, and fixed a time limit * * * to leave no room for evasion or loophole for escape, * * * the verbal amendments—to sharpen the terms—were embodied in the ultimatum, * * * and duly presented"[287]

Potsdam meeting kept secret

Now as to the Potsdam meeting September 14, 1914, a Berlin correspondent telegraphed to his Rotterdam paper that a Crown Council was held at Potsdam, July 5, 1914 July 19, 1917, Herr Haase, German minority Socialist leader, in the Reichstag, said "What the peace resolution says of the origin of the war is not tenable in fact or in history * * * We do not forget the conference at Berlin on July 5, 1914" This was published only in the *Leipziger Volkszeitung*, the next morning, the allusion to this meeting was suppressed in the reports of the Reichstag proceedings, published in other German papers No member of the German Government, then challenged the statement

Participants

With these clues, a *London Times* reporter, July 27, 1917, ascertained that there was such a meeting held, a week after the murder of the Archduke, Franz Ferdinand "Those who took part in the conference were the Emperor, his Chancellor von Bethemann-Hollweg, Admiral Tirpitz, General Falkenhaven, Mr Von Strumm, Count Berchtold Count Tisza, the Austrian and Hungarian Premiers, General Conrad von Hoetzendorf, the chief of the Austro-Hungarian staff They discussed and settled the chief points of the ultimatum that Austria was to send, eighteen days later, to Serbia," it was recognized that Russia would object, that war would result but it was definitely decided to accept this, the date of mobilization was probably fixed, the Kaiser left for Norway to throw dust in the eyes of France and Russia Two months before, at a secret meeting of the Budget Committee of the Reichstag, a Socialist member, Cohn, challenged the minister to deny

---

287 "A Scrap of Paper" by E J Dillon 1914 pp 75-77

these facts, but he did not do so. August 1, 1917, the German Government issued an official denial, and authorized the Wolff Bureau to declare "these statements and all the details were pure invention; that neither on the day named, nor any other day in July did such a conference occur either with or without the Emperor, and that the Government was completely ignorant of the contents of the ultimatum before its despatch."[288]

Denied by German government

But since then a *fuller account* of this meeting has been given by Mr. Morgenthau, American Ambassador at Constantinople, who had it first hand from Baron Wangenheim, German Ambassador at Constantinople, who attended the meeting at the summons of the Kaiser. Mr. Morganthau says: "This meeting took place at Potsdam, July 5, (1914), the Kaiser presided, nearly all the ambassadors attended. Wangenheim came to tell of Turkey * * * Molkte, chief of staff, was there representing the army, and Admiral von Tirpitz spoke for the navy. The great bankers, railroad directors and captains of German industry, all of whom were as necessary to German war preparations as the army itself, also attended. Wangenheim now told me that the Kaiser solemnly put the question to each man in turn. Was he ready for war? All replied, "Yes," except the financiers. They said that they must have two weeks to sell their foreign securities and to make loans. This conference * * * decided to give the bankers time to readjust their finances for the coming war, and then the several members went quietly back to their work or started on vacations. The Kaiser went to Norway in his yacht. Von Bethmann-Hollweg left for a rest, and Wangenheim returned to Constantinople. In telling me about this conference Wangenheim, of course, admitted that Germany precipitated the war. I think he was rather proud of the whole performance * * * * The conspiracy that has caused this greatest of human tragedies was hatched by the Kaiser and his imperial crew at the Potsdam conference of July 5, 1914."[289]

Morgenthau's first hand information

Kaiser directs

All these matters have been lately more fully confirmed if possible, by the publication of *Prince Lichnowsky's* "My London Mission, 1912-1914," prepared by him in August, 1916, "for his family archives," but copies of which were furnished to a few friends, including the head of the Hamburg-American Line, the head of the Deutsche Bank, the editor of the Berliner Tageblatt, and to an officer connected with the German General Staff. Through a breach of confidence his statement was made public. Prince Lichnowsky was German Ambassador to England, for the two years immediately preceding the commencement of the war. Among many other things he says: "I learned that at the decisive conversation at Potsdam on July 5, the inquiry

Confirmation by German ambassador to England

288. Phil. Pub. Ledger, Monday, August 6, 1917, p. 2. Facts about the War. No. 66, August, 1917.
289. World's Work, June, 1918, pp. 170-171.

addressed to us by Vienna found absolute assent among all the persons in authority, indeed they added that there would be no harm if war with Russia were to result So at any rate it is stated in the Austrian protocol which Count Mensdorf, Austrian Ambassador, received in London Soon after Herr von Jagow was in Vienna to discuss everything with Count Berchtold, Austrian Foreign Minister ' He summarizes the whole action of Germany, as follows

Lichnowsky's summary

"As appears from all official publications, without the facts being controverted by our own White Book, which, owing to its poverty and gaps, constitutes a grave self-accusation

1 "We encouraged Count Berchtold to attack Servia, although no German interest was involved, and the danger of a world war must have been known to us,—whether we knew the text of the ultimatum is a question of complete indifference"

2 "In the days before July 23, and July 30, 1914, when M Sazonof emphatically declared that Russia could not tolerate an attack on Servia, we rejected the British proposals of mediation, although Servia, under Russian and British pressure, had accepted almost the whole ultimatum, and although an agreement about the two points in question could easily have been reached, and Count Berchtold was even ready to satisfy himself with the Servian reply"

3 "On July 30, when Count Berchtold wanted to give way, we, without Austria having been attacked, replied to Russia's mere mobilization by sending an ultimatum to St Petersburg, and on July 31, we declared war on the Russians, although the Czar had pledged his word that as long as negotiations continued, not a man should march,—so that we deliberately destroyed the possibility of a peaceful settlement"

"In view of these indisputable facts, it is not surprising that the whole civilized world outside Germany attributes to us the sole guilt for the World War"[290]

Germany's bad faith

And Dr Dernburg, formerly the Kaiser's personal representative in this country, correctly characterizes Germany's bad faith when he says "Our lies are coarse and improbable, our ambiguity is pitiful simplicity, and our intrigues are without salt and without grace The history of this war proves this by a hundred examples"[291]

Truly this war was "made in Germany" and nowhere else

Austria urged by Germany, precipitated the conflict for the domination of the Balkans,—but at the last moment drew back, *Germany* then forced the war for her own schemes of world dominion, *Russia* honorably came to the rescue of a weak, kindred nation, but at the

290 New York Times April 21, 1918
291 In Deutsche Politik, September 28, 1917, War Cyclopedia, p 112

same time had important interests of her own to preserve and protect, *France*, valiant and glorious, rushed to the defence of her rights and her liberty, *England*, for her own honor, and likewise to preserve her own interests, nobly came to the aid of Belgium, France and Russia

But Belgium?—with her little army, and her forts without modern equipment,—in the eighteen days of her agony from Liege to Mons, she stemmed the onrush of the Hun deluge, until France could revise her plan of defense, and the little army of English heroes could reach the battle line Belgium! disinterested Belgium! In the dim watches of the night, from Sunday 7 p m to Monday 7 a m, August 2-3, 1914,—with her peace, her prosperity, her safety, and her life itself, on one side, and her honor on the other,—chose honor, and the cross,—and was crucified,—even as Christ of old,—that the rest of us might be free Henceforth her hallowed land shall be the Gethsemane of the Nations,—and all the world looks forward, with hope, for the day of her resurrection

And what of Germany? "Belshazzar, the king, made a great feast to a thousand of his lords They drank wine and praised the gods of gold, and of silver, of brass, of iron, of wood, and of stone And fingers of a man's hand wrote upon the plaster of the wall of the kings palace *Mene;* God hath numbered thy kingdom and finished it *Tekel;* Thou art weighed in the balances and found wanting" "Babylon the great is fallen, is fallen, and is become the habitation of devils and the hold of every foul spirit and a cage for every unclean and hateful bird her sins have reached unto heaven and God hath remembered her iniquities Therefore shall her plagues come in one day, death and mourning and famine . and the merchants of the earth shall weep and mourn over her, for no man buyeth their merchandise any more cinnamon and odors and ointments and frankincense and wine and oil and fine flour and wheat and beasts and sheep and horses and chariots and slaves and the souls of men" Dan V, 1-27, Rev XVIII, 2 et seq